HURST MEMORIAL LIBRARY
Pacific Christian College
2500 E. Nutwood
Fullerton, CA 92631

FEED MY SHEEP

A MANUAL FOR
SUNDAY SCHOOL TEACHERS,
SUPERINTENDENTS,
AND LEADERS

COMPILED AND EDITED BY
JOHN H. SCHAAL

BAKER BOOK HOUSE
GRAND RAPIDS, MICHIGAN

Copyright © 1972
by Baker Book House Company

ISBN: 0-8010-7958-6

Printed in the United States of America

FEED MY SHEEP

"So when they had broken their fast, Jesus saith to Simon Peter, Simon, son of John, lovest thou me more than these? He saith unto him, Yea, Lord; thou knowest that I love thee. He saith unto him, Feed my lambs. He saith to him again a second time, Simon, son of John, lovest thou me? He saith unto him, Yea, Lord; thou knowest that I love thee. He saith unto him, Tend my sheep. He saith unto him the third time, Simon, son of John, lovest thou me? Peter was grieved because he said unto him the third time, Lovest thou me? And he said unto him, Lord, thou knowest all things; thou knowest that I love thee. Jesus saith unto him, Feed my sheep."

John 21:15-17

FEED MY LAMBS

Feed my lambs, my son, feed my sheep;
If you love me, do not sleep,
In the fields, my son, work and weep;
Feed my lambs, my son, feed my sheep.

Charles A. Buffham

© *Copyright 1969 by Singspiration, Inc.*
All rights reserved. Used by permission.

PREFACE

Feed My Sheep is a publication of the Midwest Sunday School Association, a book that has resulted from the success of the first work issued by the Association back in 1947. The original, titled *Feed My Lambs,* was the product of an essay contest on Sunday school improvement. The original edition of less than twelve hundred copies was soon sold out; and because persistent demand for the book or a replacement continued during the intervening twenty-five years, this second book is now being presented.

Feed My Sheep aims to fulfill the need and request for guidance and instruction in organizing and conducting a successful Sunday school. It strives to assist those superintendents and teachers who have had little or no professional experience or training in teaching, yet have a desire to serve as Christian workers and witnesses in spreading the gospel message. It is written to a generation that is keenly aware of the challenge to the church and kingdom because of the increasing problems, strong demoniac influences, and rapidly changing values confronting us. This book will prove helpful to those who are eager to equip themselves in the best possible way to teach God's will through Christ and the Holy Spirit.

Feed My Sheep contains contributed articles in the area of professional knowledge, solicited manuscripts, one reprint from the first book, and a potpourri chapter of miscellaneous items—including a sample constitution—for which there have been frequent requests. One chapter is devoted to the mission Sunday school to help those working with people outside the sphere of the church; and still another deals with covenantal thinking as it applies to the Sunday school.

In my capacity as editor I was given the freedom to obtain the writers and articles. I am indebted to the contributors for their cooperation and willingness to write, to the many helpful suggestions received from typists and readers, and particularly to Marvin Bolt, the executive secretary, and the officers of the Midwest Sunday School Association, both past and present. They have encouraged me and assumed the final responsibility of producing this volume.

It is the genuine prayer and joyous hope of all of us who have had a part in this venture that God will use *Feed My Sheep* as an effective tool in promoting His kingdom. Through it may the Sunday school gain pupils who will be led to the Lord Jesus Christ, be taught more effectively, and be used in His kingdom for many years of consecrated service.

John H. Schaal
Dean and Bible Teacher
The Reformed Bible College
Grand Rapids, Michigan

CONTENTS

1 The School We Need 11
   Joel Nederhood

2 Sunday School Is Worthwhile 19
   John F. De Vries

3 Creative Teaching 31
   Marchiene Rienstra

4 Understanding Our Sunday School Children 43
   Katie Gunnink

5 Sunday School—An Evangelism Arm of the Church . 51
   Henry Hoekstra

6 The Sunday School Superintendent 59
   Wendell J. Schaal

7 The Sunday School Teacher—A Look at Yourself ... 65
   John H. Schaal

Contents

8 Preschoolers—Miniature Adults? 75
   Eileen Van't Kerkhoff

9 Building and Using the Church Library for
   Sunday School 85
   Joanne Boehm

10 Seeing Is Believing—Look at and Learn from
   Visual Aids 95
   Elaine Mannes and Jennie De Roos

11 Seeing Is Believing—Helps and Hints
   for Visual Aids 103
   Elaine Mannes and Jennie De Roos

12 The Family's Involvement in the Sunday School ... 113
   Marilyn J. Schaal

13 Praising the Lord with Music 121
   Carole Zinger

14 Sunday School Management 131
   James P. Hoekenga

15 From the Editor's Scrapbook 147

THE SCHOOL WE NEED

Joel Nederhood

The seventies could be the decade of the Sunday school. There are several considerations that prompt this suggestion.

It is significant that both youth and adults are looking for ways to supplement the regular worship service. A good many of them agree that nothing should ever take the place of the obedient gathering of the congregation beneath the proclamation of the Word. That moment is too essential a part of the deepest nature of the church for any major changes. Nevertheless there is growing agreement that most people need and deserve something in addition. People need something less formal than organized worship services tend to be, and less authoritarian. People need a place where they can probe more, talk more, give and take more.

Sunday school already fills this bill and could do so even more, given creative attention. Perhaps its name might have to be changed in some circumstances and a bit more responsiveness to the needs of those who attend it built in. But there are no reasons, aside from the ruts we are in, why

---

Joel Nederhood, Chicago, Illinois, is the radio pastor of the Back to God Hour heard weekly over an international network.

Sunday school could not develop into what many are looking for: that mysterious, illusive structure that is close to the church, but isn't quite the same as a regular worship service.

And there is another factor that could work in favor of the Sunday school. That is the increased leisure time already enjoyed by many and which should characterize life more and more during the remainder of this decade. The long weekend, the four-day week, long vacations, early retirement, and even involuntary periodic unemployment will free people from regular job demands. For some, these conditions will impose an intolerable burden of boredom. But these conditions also have their positive dimension.

The opening up of large segments of time for creative use is a challenge to the church. A person who has Friday and Saturday to water-ski every week of the summer instead of just Saturday afternoon might conceivably get tired enough of his recreation to become interested in what the church has to offer. This could happen especially if his life is invaded by a crisis of one kind or another. At this point a vital Sunday school program becomes extremely important, for it is especially useful in serving the more or less casual inquirer. In any case, the increase of leisure time could work to the advantage of the Sunday school by providing candidates of all ages who would enjoy filling their time with the study that would equip them to be teachers.

There is, therefore, no compelling reason to mourn the demise of the Sunday school, for if the new opportunities are seized and creative responses are maintained, church activities in general and Sunday school in particular could flourish. But this will happen in fact only if new levels of enthusiasm for the institution of Sunday school are generated. This can happen if we see clearly where Sunday school fits into the total program of the church and when we understand the specific contribution it can make to the church's total well-being.

Well, how does the Sunday school fit into the total program of the church? Let's try to determine this, first of all, by way of contrast. As an educational event, Sunday school competes with the proclamation of the Word in worship and with the official instruction given in the catechism program. In many locales it also competes with what is done in Christian school Bible courses.

Sunday school differs from the official proclamation of the Word and from catechism in terms of *authority*. Sunday school is nonauthoritarian; that is, it is not an official expression of church teaching. It is freer. It is more responsive. It is more open to question and dialogue.

Compared to Bible instruction in the Christian day school, Sunday school is nonacademic. It's not just that there are no tests in Sunday school, but the Biblical material is handled with greater attention to the moral and ethical truths than is generally done in the more rigidly structured knowledge blocks that make up the Christian school Bible curriculums.

These distinctions and contrasts do not hold at every point, but they are sufficiently real to establish that the Sunday school has a unique role to play within the life of God's people. What that role is precisely can best be highlighted by saying that Sunday school is *a specific expression of the communion of the saints*. This makes it extremely important, for the communion of the saints was from the beginning of the church's life considered important enough to merit special mention in the Apostles' Creed. Sunday school expresses in a particularly happy way the answer given to Question 55 of the Heidelberg Catechism, for it is a place where the members of the body of Christ can cheerfully employ their several gifts for the mutual enrichment of the entire church. If Sunday school is seen in terms of the communion of the saints, its importance is immediately clarified and possibilities for its effective use become limited only by our imagination.

As an expression of the communion of the saints, Sunday school is the place where our children can learn about Jesus from the lips of a housewife whom they see occasionally in the grocery store, or from the same man who delivers milk to their door. It is the place where children can speak frankly to someone who is their parents' age, but to whom they can say things they would not perhaps say to their parents. It is also the place where adults, meeting together on a more or less equal basis, can testify to each other and sharpen each other's spiritual perception.

Now, if Sunday school is in fact an important expression of the communion of the saints, there are several observations which become rather obvious. First of all, it merits the continuous interest of the church. That is, there should be a thriving Sunday school program all year round. It is unfortunate that there are churches that have Sunday school simply because most other churches have them, and that is about the only reason for their existence. The actual Sunday school program is conducted without enthusiasm, as a very marginal event that is surrounded by the aura of defeatism and low morale. This is expressed in the failure of such churches to maintain a Sunday school program throughout the year. Sometimes the Sunday school season ends by the first of June and doesn't resume until the first of October. This means that on twenty-five to thirty percent of the Sundays there is no Sunday school at all. This gives the impression that Sunday school is not all that important, and church members cannot be blamed if their level of interest is very superficial and gradually deteriorates.

Furthermore, the failure to maintain a year-round Sunday school program will render that program quite useless as a tool for reaching the community. As we shall see later, Sunday school is especially well equipped to extend a church's ministry to members of the community who are not church members. But if it is not even available twenty-five percent of the year, community people cannot be expected to develop significant interest in it. The failure of a Sunday school to be open during the summer has made it impossible for many a church to capitalize on its summer Bible school enrollment. Community children who have attended a church's Bible school but who have to wait two months before the church's Sunday school begins, probably will not attend that church's Sunday school.

The high importance of Sunday school suggests, too, doesn't it, that it should involve all the members of a congregation? Obviously, children cannot be expected to take Sunday school very seriously if they observe that their parents couldn't care less about it. Adult classes are therefore very necessary if the full potential of the Sunday school is to be felt in a congregation's life. The Sunday school needs adults in order to project a well-rounded program. But the adults need the Sunday school, too, as much as any other group. Possibly they need it more. The adult classes will be there for the parents of nonchurched children to attend; and that, too, is another reason why any Sunday school that does not have a well-developed adult program will be crippled.

For churches that have never had adult programs, the introduction of such activity must overcome considerable built-in resistance in most cases. Perhaps it is necessary to down-play the schoolish dimension of Sunday school, stressing that the fact that we call it a school is conditioned by history more than anything else. It dates back to the time when children who had to work in factories learned their arithmetic in such schools on Sunday. The school idea tends to suggest that people beyond school age should be excused from the obligation to attend. Actually, Sunday school is a very versatile structure that can be tailored to meet the needs of every group within the church. If it is a school at all, it is a school with a very adaptable quality.

On the lower levels, where children are still fascinated by the story aspect of many of the Biblical episodes and are not bored with the repetition of this material, Sunday school will be very similar to a child's early school experiences. Since the school experience as such is new to the child, he will not resent the similarity between Sunday school and day school. And he will benefit from the factual knowledge he acquires in Sunday school at this age.

As the age level in the classes advances, the structure of the Sunday school should gradually be modified from the class type situation in the direction of discussion until, finally, on the adult level, the teacher (or leader) and the participants will stand on an equal footing and will, in a large degree, share insights and comments. In the teen-age classes, the teacher will retain much of his direction-giving role; but already at that point he will often find himself functioning as a discussion leader. As this process works itself out naturally, what happens in these young people's classes will develop into fine expressions of Christian conversation in the adult classes. The conversation will not be random nor undisciplined, since it will center on a single topic or passage of Scripture. But it will be conversation, nonetheless, with every member contributing and benefiting. At this point the communion-of-the-saints quality of the Sunday school experience will be expressed most fully.

If a church develops proper points of view regarding its Sunday school and maintains year-round classes for all ages, the Sunday school will be in a position to contribute a great deal to the total life of the church. This contribution could be described from various angles. But most of them can be included in noting that a properly operating Sunday school is particularly well equipped to be the vestibule—the entry way—to the church. It is the entry way to worship on the Lord's Day for the regular member of the church. And it is the entry way into the very life of the church for the nonchurched people who gradually work their way into a local church by participating in the Sunday school first. It is, incidentally, this function of the Sunday school that makes it imperative that Sunday school be held before the worship service, not after. If it is held before the worship service it can be a church's front door. If it meets afterward, it will be the back door—an exit, not an entrance.

In order to understand the important function of the Sunday school as the entry way into the church, we need simply notice that for all its importance, a formal worship service has at least a couple of disadvantages that probably won't go away for awhile. The very importance of the worship service, which must remain the high point in the congregation's life, surrounds it with a rather formidable quality that the outsider finds difficult to crack. The congregation sits rather formally and follows a prescribed order of worship. And when the members leave, not a great deal is said within the church itself. People who know one another find each other for conversation, but a stranger feels left out.

In addition, the formal worship service needs a little preparation among those who attend regularly as well. The big change from our ordinary pace during the week to what happens in church is sometimes just a little more than a man's frazzled spirit can bear. Sunday school can help people make this adjustment. A congregation that has been prepared for the preaching of the Word through prior attendance at Sunday school will be more receptive than one that has hastened to church at an early hour and which waits to see what the minister has to offer before they rush off to have coffee with their friends.

The ability of a Sunday school to prepare the church members for worship makes it extremely attractive. But its ability to perform this service for those who are essentially unacquainted with the life of the church makes it doubly so. It can be the entry way into the church for the nonchurched, who use it to sample the church's life before committing themselves more fully to participating in it. Nonchurched parents can often be convinced that they should send their children to a Sunday school. After the children have attended for some time, the parents can be invited to Sunday school too. This will seem natural to them. And even if adult friends have no children in a church's Sunday school, church members can invite them more easily to Sunday school than to church, for most non-church goers consider Sunday school attendance less compromising than church attendance. Once these adults start coming to Sunday school, they will be able to test the sincerity level of their peers who are members of the church and they will gradually develop friendships. As this process advances, it will finally become almost natural for them to attend the regular worship services. When they finally do—and this process may be as short as three weeks or as long as three years—they will be going to church with their friends.

It is the ability of the Sunday school to function as the entry way into the church for people who are presently outside it, that makes it so necessary that it develop into an increasingly strong element of the church's life in the years ahead. But it is essential before this can be done that the church be vitally interested in expanding its circle of ministry. Churches that consistently demonstrate that their interests are largely provincial and that continue to exhibit the marks of a private club, probably would do better to forget the Sunday school altogether. It will only be a bother to them and will probably cause more problems than they would care to put up with. At the same time, such churches, encrusted with attitudes so brittle, would probably barely qualify as the living church of the Lord Jesus Christ.

A local church, on the other hand, that is astonished by the salvation that has been revealed through Jesus Christ and that is thunderstruck by the universal intention of God in bringing this gospel to all the world and every social class, will feel compelled to make use of every means available to reach all men with the gospel. For such a church, Sunday school will become an exceptionally exciting tool of evangelism. And with that, it will provide the regular members of the church with enrichment that will pay off with abundant spiritual dividends for the entire communion of the saints.

Sunday school is the school we need for times like these. The question is, Do we have the living faith, the driving ambition, and the grand integrity to use it well in the years ahead? If the answer is negative, the reflection is on us, not on this good tool God has given us. Since we are working for a God of judgment, it behooves us to work hard at making Sunday school increasingly useful, starting now.

2 SUNDAY SCHOOL IS WORTHWHILE

John F. De Vries

Sunday schools are up against it! They face some pretty stiff competition. They are manned by amateur teachers who cannot begin to compete with the professional teachers our children have in their day schools. The time period of Sunday school is limited to a short forty-five-minute period once a week, and the class is usually held under anything but ideal conditions. And, if this is not enough, consider for a moment the plight of the poor Sunday school teacher whose children attend a Christian day school. The weekly Sunday school class becomes some kind of game in which the teacher, in a forty-five-minute period, is supposed to present something new and exciting about a Bible story which the children probably had recently in a very thorough way, in their Christian day school. One of the greatest frustrations many Sunday school teachers face is the bored comment by the class when a new story is introduced— "Oh, we just had that in school!"

Because of this, many have begun to entertain doubts

John F. De Vries, South Holland, Illinois, is the director of Bible Correspondence for the World Home Bible League.

about the effectiveness of Sunday school in educating children. What is its place? What role does it play? Should we just scrap it as a tradition of the past—something to be discarded in modern times? How can we expect amateur teachers to compete with professionals, especially when they have only forty-five minutes a week to teach, and then teach in something far less than adequate conditions?

Can anything be done? Can the Sunday school occupy a uniquely important place in our church life? Can it be removed from competition with the day school, so that its role is excitingly different? Can we find some way to teach both the children from the community and our own Christian children—many of whom attend Christian day schools—in the same class, at the same time? Shouldn't we just be honest with ourselves and throw out this archaic institution and begin to search for something that is tailored to modern times?

I want to suggest that, in spite of seemingly insurmountable odds, the Sunday school can occupy a worthwhile place in the life of the church. Some changes will have to be made, but the Sunday school exists as the one organization in our church life which can fill one of the vacuums in our educational structure.

Let's examine our goals in the Sunday school. What are we trying to do? Obviously, we are trying to teach children from two kinds of backgrounds: the homes of church members and the homes of people living in the community who may or may not be Christian. These children approach the Bible from widely divergent points of view. Is it possible to teach both groups in the same class, capturing their interest and challenging them? I think so. Let's look first at the children of the church and then we will examine the children from the community.

The children of the church

They sit there on Sunday morning, these children of the church, children whose parents are regular members of the congregation, and they wait for the teacher to enter. Who are they? Tiny lions waiting to taunt the teacher, to test and threaten him, or her, for forty-five minutes to see who is the stronger? Unfortunately, some teachers fall into the rut of thinking of their class in such terms and feel that they have been successful if only they made it through the hour with some semblance of discipline.

As a teacher approaches his class, he should remember four things about these children. First of all, each child is an immortal soul. These are living persons called into existence six, ten, or fourteen years ago by an almighty God and they will never cease to exist. That's a rather frightening and sobering thought, and every teacher should be conscious of it as he enters the classroom. We have been entrusted with the teaching of creatures who will live for all eternity. They are not numbers or names, or little ogres there to taunt you and test your ability to regulate the discipline of your classroom. Instead, they are immortal souls, seeking guidance from you concerning the spiritual welfare of the life that has begun within them.

The next thing we should remember about these children of the church is that they are not only immortal souls, but they are immortal souls deeply loved by almighty God. As a matter of fact, there is nothing more precious in the sight of God than these little creatures who sit before us on a Sunday morning. It may be hard to imagine at times; but they are creatures created in the image of God and resemble Him with their minds, personalities, wills, and creative abilities. They are so precious to God that He has paid for them with the life of His only begotten Son. They have become the precious possessions of God! God is jealous of them, and warns us severely that if we let one of them stumble or turn from Him, it would be better for us that we did not exist, or that a millstone were hung around our neck and we were cast out into the middle of the sea! God places in the hands of a Sunday school teacher, every Sunday morning, His greatest possession, the little lives for which His only Son suffered and died!

We must remember a third thing about these children of the church: they are children of the promise. You are dealing with crown princes and princesses—children who are destined to share in the inheritance which God reserved for His only Son; children who are destined some day to rule the universe and judge the angels. God has set before them a treasure house of promises; and it is the task of the Sunday school teacher to unlock the vault and lead the children in, showing them that all things will work for their good; that they can have power to move mountains; that regardless of the afflictions which they face, they will not be hurt. The Sunday school teacher is to awaken within them the realization that they are crown princes and princesses and that no one in all the world has the privileges, promises, and wealth available to them that they have.

One more consideration. These children of the church are children of great responsibility! From those to whom much is given, much is required. There isn't anyone quite so nauseating as the person coming from an extremely wealthy family, who has had all the advantages of the best education in the world, and who then squanders it all by becoming a playboy. But our churches are rapidly being filled with "spiritual playboys"—children who have had everything, but who are concerned only about their own personal pleasures. They are thrill seekers of the first order and suffer an acute case of "I" disease. We have trained many of them to conceive of the church as an agency designed to serve them in their spiritual life; and so they come to church to get something out of it, rather than coming to bring something of themselves in praise to God and service to their fellowman. The Sunday school teacher is in a unique position to impress upon these children that they have greater responsibilities than any other child living today.

What must we do with them?

Four things: the first task which uniquely, although certainly not exclusively, belongs to the Sunday school teacher is that of impressing upon these children of the church the necessity for a daily, conscious commitment of their lives to Jesus Christ. Obviously, this is to be done in all areas—the home, the Christian day school, the catechism class. But in a special way, I think, it belongs in the Sunday school. These forty-five-minute classes should be training sessions in the art of living in a conscious relationship with Jesus Christ, rather than trying to repeat Bible stories heard during the week or trying to repeat doctrinal matters taught in catechism. Few laymen realize the tremendous psychological advantage they enjoy in talking about deeply personal, spiritual matters—an advantage over the pastor and professional teacher who are paid to do these things. Here in the Sunday school class our children should be trained in ways in which the Holy Spirit can possess them and use them. Beginning already in the third and fourth grades, the forte of the Sunday school class should lie in the fact that it is a period in which practical, day-to-day Christianity is discussed and considered on the specific age level of the child.

The second goal in regard to the children of the church is to teach them how to read the Bible and apply it to their lives. The failure of both the catechism program and the Christian day school in this area is one of the greatest tragedies of our church. We have a denomination of people who have never been taught how to read the Bible and apply it to their lives in a practical, day-to-day way. If the Sunday school would see this as its central task regarding the children of the church, in very close conjunction with the first goal stated above, the Sunday school would suddenly find a wonderful new place in the life of our churches. Let the Sunday school become the place where our children are trained to read the Bible, where they are trained in the art of private devotions.

This goal can be carried out in a rather simple way. We need not change the structure of our curriculum—merely the methods used to teach this material. May I suggest a very simple technique to attain this goal?

1. Have the children sit in a circle and read the Bible passage for the week aloud. (Use a modern translation—an absolute must!) After they have read the passage, ask each student to put a verse into his or her own words and again go

around the circle. Build this up in the student's mind by calling it a "Translating session."

2. After you have paraphrased the passage, ask the students whether there is anything in the passage which they don't understand. Don't be too hasty in offering your own explanation. Make them wrestle through it.

3. Now begin to search for the lessons from this passage. What does it teach us about practical Christian life? Ask them to make a "sermon" on the passage. Again, do not be hasty in trying to help them; but attempt gently to force them to do this themselves. Lead them into the general challenges by asking questions designed to point out the lessons contained in the material.

4. Next, try to select a key verse from the material—one which should become your memory text. Your students should be encouraged to repeat this daily throughout the week.

5. Finally, have a prayer session. Write the lessons and challenges of the passage on a blackboard; then, in a prayer session, ask God to help each one carry out these things in his life. Discuss the answers to prayer which God has sent during the previous week.

The Sunday school can occupy a third unique role in our church as the training ground for the reception of unchurched people into our fellowship. Our people must be trained in the gracious reception of those from the community who are interested in attending our church. They must be training in the art of making strangers feel at home without "falling all over them" and scaring them away. The Sunday school, when properly used, provides the right organization in which this can be done. The children can be trained in actual life situations by the example of the teacher in how to receive community children and make them feel at home. Some sessions of Sunday school (when the unchurched are absent) should be devoted exclusively to lessons on this subject.

Finally, the Sunday school can occupy a unique role in

instilling in our children a consciousness of witnessing. This can be done in a number of different ways. Campaigns to bring unchurched friends and neighbors to Sunday school should be conducted on a regular basis. Sunday school classes should occasionally take part in a simple door-to-door literature distribution campaign. One of the things that stands out most clearly in my mind concerning Sunday school is the practice of distributing a special tract each Easter and Christmas to all the homes in our community. The older children in the Sunday school can very effectively canvass the community, offering a home Bible study course.

In summary, the Sunday school, as far as the children of the church are concerned, occupies a unique role in the fact that it, more than any other agency, is designed to teach a child how to read the Bible and apply it to his life, to train the child in the art of receiving the unchurched into the fellowship of the church, and to instill in the child a burning desire to share the gospel with others.

The children of the community

If we had only one type of child in the Sunday school class—either the child of the church or the child of the community—much of our problem concerning Sunday school would be solved. But when we begin to mix children from divergent backgrounds in the same class, problems do arise. The Bible lesson can be fascinating for the child who has never heard it, while for the child from the church it tends to be boring and repetitious. How can we place children with almost no Scriptural background in the same class with children from Christian homes?

Perhaps we can give a partial answer to this problem by analyzing who the children of the community are, and what we expect to do for them in Sunday school.

Who are the children of the neighborhood who sporadically attend our Sunday school classes? The first thing we should remember as we think of these children is that they too, like the children of the church, are immortal creatures made in the image and likeness of God and they are destined never to stop existing. When facing children it is absolutely necessary that we never lose sight of the greatness and sacredness of the human being; God has entrusted the care of the greatest creatures in the universe to us! These children of the neighborhood who come to hear God's Word at our church are children who are deeply loved by God, for God gives us every indication in His Word that He desires that they be saved. We are told that the angels of heaven rejoice when one of these little ones turns to Christ and accepts Him as personal Lord and Savior. Seldom did our Savior grow as angry as when He rebuked His disciples for refusing mothers the opportunity to bring their little children to Him. As Sunday school teachers we are commissioned by God to communicate His love for these children by our words and by our example of personal interest in their lives. Each child must come to feel the deep respect which the teacher has for him—a respect which can be achieved only in the knowledge that this child is an immortal being, created in the image of God and deeply loved by God.

We must remember a second thing about the child from the neighborhood: he is a child over whom a tremendous battle is raging. We are prone to forget the other race of intelligent creatures who inhabit the universe and who are deeply concerned about the ultimate outcome of this battle. Satan and his hosts will not sit idly by and watch a child like this come to church or Sunday school on a regular basis. The Sunday school teacher must realize that as this child begins to attend and show interest in the Word of God, Satan will be there to disrupt and trouble his life. He will be doing all he can to discourage the child from attending regularly. He will try to make the teacher indifferent to the child's needs and the regularity of his attendance. He will try to cause trouble and tension in the child's home in an attempt to keep him from attending with any regularity. It is good to anticipate these problems and be prepared to meet them. Remember that the child who comes from the unchurched home in your community is the subject of a fantastic battle in the spirit world as Satan and his powers attempt to prevent that child from hearing the gospel.

As we think of the child of the neighborhood we must remember a third thing: this child is the doorway to an unchurched family. The child cannot be viewed merely as an individual. Child evangelism that is divorced from any attempts to reach the parents with the gospel is for the most part a rather futile exercise and will produce few lasting results. God didn't make Junior the head of the home, even though many people today seem to think so. The fact that this child is enrolled in your class gives you a natural opening with the family; but, unfortunately, many teachers do not use it. Your task is not merely to teach the child, but to reach through this child to his parents and attempt to get them into a regular, systematic study of the Word of God. Seldom has a child been able to continue in a commitment to Christ if the home remains antireligious. Parents who have little or nothing to do with religion, even though they may permit their children to attend Sunday school, will ultimately destroy most of what the child learns on Sunday until they are personally convinced of the truth of Christianity and are led to give their lives to Christ.

What must we do with the children of the community? What goals should we have in mind for them? The first and most important goal is, of course, to introduce the child of the community to Jesus Christ and call him to make a conscious, daily commitment of his life to Christ as his Savior and Lord. This can best be done, for both the child of the church and the child of the community, by rather frequent references to the plan of salvation taken from the Book of Romans. The entire class should be required to memorize this and be able to recite it and explain it. It consists of four very simple verses: Romans 3:23; 6:23, 5:8; and 3:24, 25. (All these verses should be taken from the Living New Testament for the sake of clarity and simplicity.) Go over these verses with your class, pointing out as simply as you can the basic facts of salvation. Encourage them to share this with their unsaved neighbors and friends. Perhaps you may wish to present them with their own copy of the New Testament in which some of these verses are underlined.

The second goal regarding the children of the community is to train them in the art of reading the Bible and applying it to their lives. Perhaps the greatest problem of the Sunday school lies in the fact that we are trying to teach children from widely divergent backgrounds. The disproportionate amount of knowledge represented in the child of the church and the child of the community forms a rather formidable barrier to effective teaching. The Bible stories, so new and interesting to the one group, are old hat to the other group. However, when the Sunday school becomes the instrument which the church uses in training children how to read the Bible and apply it to their lives, this wide divergence in background no longer seems to be such a great liability. Both groups of children are placed on the same level. You are not trying to teach a story so much as to discuss a story and arrive at some general conclusions concerning its teaching for your practical life. Both groups are placed on the same level, and both groups are engaged in the excitement of discovering that the Bible does speak in a very practical, meaningful way in our lives.

The third goal should be to introduce the child of the community to the love and concern of the Christians in the church. Everything should be done to make the child feel accepted, loved, and part of a fellowship of believers. The teacher must try to get him to experience some of the thrill of belonging to this unique group of people in the world—the Christian church. This is one area in which our churches have failed to a great degree. It is one thing to witness, one thing to spread literature, one thing to pay for radio time, but it is an entirely different matter to receive a person from the community and impart to him the feeling of fellowship and belonging which the church must always offer. One distinctive thing about the New Testament church was the fellowship which it enjoyed. And in this age of division and revolution this is one of the greatest experiences which the church can offer to our lonely world—a place where you can belong and feel at home, regardless of who you are and what you have done. We should be much in prayer that our Sunday school classes afford that type of Christian fellowship and sense of belonging which attracts the child of the community and encourages regular attendance.

The final goal which we should have regarding the child of the community is to reach out through this child to his family. In a certain sense child evangelism exists only as a means to enter the child's family with the gospel of Jesus Christ. No Sunday school teacher should ever be content with merely instructing a child. He must make an attempt to contact his family and to know all those involved in the child's life. By all means obtain Bible courses written just for the non-Christian adult and use them in instructing parents of children from the community. There are courses available which can be taught by correspondence or in small groups.

The Sunday school, with certain basic changes, can be one of the most effective tools of evangelism which the church possesses. But it can be much more. The Sunday school can be the source of instruction in how to read the Bible and apply it to our daily lives. One cannot begin to imagine the fantastic change which would occur in the life of a denomination if such an approach were taken to teaching Scripture, and our young people and children would become genuinely excited about studying the Word of God. Such excitement will not be generated, however, until our children are led to discover the fact that the Bible does speak, in a practical way, to their daily lives.

3 CREATIVE TEACHING

Marchiene Rienstra

Creative teaching? you ask. How does a teacher create? Can a teacher create as artists create? Yes, a teacher can. You can. But your materials are not paint or stone or clay. They are other human beings, the great beauty and truth of the Christian faith, and certain kinds of physical materials and spaces. But it takes time and effort. You cannot imitate someone else, or simply follow well-worn patterns. To create in teaching you must master the tools and materials, use them with skill, and combine them in fresh, new ways which reflect your uniqueness as a person. And you must be flexible, open, and honest with yourself and your students. For you, there are no easy, pat answers or methods. For you, there is instead the risk and challenge of experimenting with a wide range of possibilities as you keep looking for new and better ways of using your material to teach most effectively.

As you do this, there are certain guidelines which may be of help to you. In the following pages, these will be presented

---

Marchiene Rienstra, Grand Rapids, Michigan, is the wife of Dr. John Rienstra and has served as writer and speaker for the Sunday school movement.

in terms of the four types of materials which you, as a creative teacher, must deal with. They are: 1) you and your students as individuals; 2) you and your students as a single, functioning unit; 3) your physical environment—that is, the space and equipment available to you; and 4) your subject material.

As we begin to discuss these guidelines, the obvious place to start is with you, the teacher. For the way you see yourself—the idea you have of your role—will determine how creatively you teach.

What, then, is your role as a creative teacher? It is to act as a resource person and guide; to bring out what is in your pupils, rather than to pour something into them. You must lead them along so that they can face the truths and rejoice in the beauty of the Christian faith. You cannot do this for them. They must be given the challenge to grapple personally with the truths to which you lead them, and react in their own way to the beauty you show them. Your leadership must be of the kind that witnesses to those truths which have meant the most in your life. A spirit of joy and sensitivity should pervade your teaching, so that children feel drawn by the goodness and beauty you are showing them, rather than being made to feel that this is stuff they have to believe and learn or else! This means that you do not dominate the classroom. Rather, you allow the students to explore and express their questions and answers in their own unique ways. Your job is to know as much as possible so that you can be an effective resource person for the children to come to. Your method will be to help them with their questions so that they arrive at the answers themselves rather than being given the answers by you, without any effort and struggle on their part.

As you do this, you will have to allow for the fact that some of the things you want to teach are less important than others for your students, and that some will react more fully to one kind of truth than others. Be prepared for a lot of variation and "ups and downs." The business of creating is a slow, painful one. But in the end, it accomplishes much more than any other method. And above all, remember that only God Himself can bring anyone to Him, and that the truths He wants to teach us take a lifetime to learn. You are simply one small instrument among many others that He will be using. Many of the truths in your lesson book will take your students years to learn. Many of them are still not fully learned by you and many other Christians. So have the right long-range perspective on your task. Many students will not learn what you think they should. Many will learn, but you will not know it. And few of them will probably remember very much of what you said one year from now. This is all a part of reality which God puts there to keep us humble—and perhaps to remind us that more important than any amount of lesson-teaching is the love that should exist between the teacher and each child. For long after your students have forgotten your lessons, they will remember how they felt about you and their fellow students. That memory will probably be good if you teach each of your students as a unique, special person, unlike any other.

You know that each one has his own set of problems and needs, his own strengths and weaknesses, his own peculiar way of looking at the world and you. But too often, this fact gets overlooked in the classroom, and children are taught as if they were all alike—all at the same time, with the same method, and from a background of scanty information about each child. You, as a creative teacher, can create no worthwhile teaching methods without taking each individual student into account, and loving each one as a precious, unique person created in God's image. To do that, you must know as much as you can about each child as you begin to teach.

This can be done in many ways. You can interview each child separately, asking each one about himself with the best questions you can devise (questions about their feelings and ideas as well as facts about them). You can ask each child old enough to do so to write down what he thinks are the three or four most important things about himself, and the two or three questions which are most important to him. You can talk to each child's parents about the child. You can spend a class period having children pair off and find out about each other, and then share their findings with the class. You can keep a file on each child, frequently adding your personal observations and record of his work. After all, you cannot really love a child you hardly know. The more you know, the more effectively you can love, understand, and teach that child.

First Corinthians 13 says that if we have not love, anything else we do—no matter how well—is worth nothing. This means, in terms of teaching technique—and this is important—that you will not always deal with your class as a unit. Your pupils should not always be doing the same thing at the same time. In the best classrooms all over the country today, educators are discovering that the best learning takes place when children are offered a variety of ways to learn something, and are allowed to choose their own pace and style. In a given hour in your classroom, for instance, there may be three children reading a Bible story; two or three painting a picture expressing their reaction to the lesson of the day; three or four more making up a song or verse or story in their own words expressing the truth you have witnessed to; and four or five others looking up Bible verses related to the day's story or truth. You would be circulating from group to group, person to person, helping, watching, encouraging. Of course, there are times when you should function all together as a unified group—perhaps when you pray or sing or discuss, work on a common project, study Bible passages, or take an offering (although all these things can be done in several small groups too). The important point is to get across very clearly to each child that you love and treasure him, and want to help. You attitude and comments will always, therefore, be constructive and positive, never negative and critical. Each student must feel that you are on his side, no matter how he may fail in performance or behavior.

It is also important to get your students to relate to you and each other in such a way that you function as a close, loving, accepting group of people. This, after all, is what the communion of the saints is all about. There are many ways in which you as a teacher can help this to happen, so that your students experience the meaning of the communion of the saints. Such an experience can teach them far more about the nature of the church, the importance of Christian fellowship, and the meaning of being part of God's family than all the sermons or lectures in the world. Moreover, the latest evidence in educational research shows that the best learning goes on in groups where people like and trust each other, where there is a spirit of cooperation, give and take, honesty and forgiveness, rather than the all-too-common classroom where competition, one-upmanship, and ignorance about each other prevail.

This means that you should not use grades. Rather, you should describe for each student, privately, where he is weak and strong, and point out how he can improve. Nor should you try to get children to compete with each other in order to learn a lesson better. To learn something or do something—especially a Christian truth—because it puts you a step ahead of someone else, and shows you to be superior, is entirely the wrong motive. It destroys the very thing you are trying to do—help children and young people love truth for its own sake, and apply it by helping each other, each humbly considering others better than himself (Phil. 2).

Therefore, you as a teacher need to do all you can to get all the children in your class to know, understand, appreciate, and help each other. Whatever will produce a spirit of love and unity in the group is of first importance. For it is in the context of a loving, forgiving, supporting relationship that the best learning of Christian truth can take place. In this way, your students can be made to realize that the truths they are learning must be integrated with their lives, must influence the very class they are in and the way they work together and treat each other and you. It is a great tragedy when a teacher, in eagerness to get through the lesson plan, neglects personal and group relationships. For what children pick up from such failures in our churches is that Christianity is a set of principles they have to hurry up and learn, but having little to do with their daily life and concerns.

There are many methods you can use to create the necessary good group relationship in your classroom. One obvious way is to set aside times when you encourage the children (with you leading the way by example) to share their joys, worries, problems, and questions with each other and you, and to pray together in a specific way about them. At first, there may be some tension and reluctance. But with patience, time, and determined effort and prayer on your part, you will find that these times of personal sharing and praying will become very precious and will often be the high points of your time together. And in the context of a child's concern—perhaps about a sick sister, an absent father, a troubling fear, a recent joy—Christian truth can be naturally discussed, meshed with the children's concerns, meeting them *where they are*. To do that, of course, you must be open and honest, and encourage your students to be the same. Help them to realize that fears, doubts, and resentments are all part of the nature they are created with, but that they must be dealt with in a constructive way. In doing all of this, you will find marvelous opportunities for teaching children about God's forgiveness, their need to forgive each other, the meaning and wisdom of Christian ethics—all at the time when these issues are brought up by the children themselves, and therefore important to them. So often, we as teachers will teach a lesson without regard to what is really going on inside the students that day. It is better to be ready to scrap a lesson, if necessary, in order to deal with an immediate need.

There are other interesting and effective techniques for getting your students to relate to each other. You will probably need to use them, since there is a natural defensiveness and suspicion that keeps people wary and distant. It takes real planning and effort to destroy those barriers. You must be sensitive to the existence of such barriers in your class too, and gently and lovingly work at helping the children to overcome them. One way is to ask each student to pick someone at random and then show somehow, without words, that he loves the other person. This is a good place to show that love is not primarily a feeling, but a decision of the will to be on the side of the other person in spite of everything. Another way is to pick one person and ask others to tell something they like about him. Turns can be taken with such a game so everyone gets an opportunity to build others up and be built up himself. If there is something children don't like about each other, that too can be talked about constructively in terms of mutual tolerance and forgiveness.

Another good technique is called role playing. This is often a good way to get children to get inside a certain Bible story or truth and also to express their own reactions. For example, one teacher asked two boys who frequently fought with each other to act out the Bible story of Cain and Abel twice. First one was Cain and the other was Abel, and then the other way around. Afterwards, the class discussed the destructive consequences of hatred and the need for mutual love and forgiveness. It profoundly affected the two boys, who got along much better after that. The teacher said very little that day, but she did a great deal of creative teaching. So, experiment with spontaneous play acting and role playing as you deal with stories and parables from the Bible. Let children also create their own brief "situation plays" to present a truth. One teacher, for example, had her class divide into teams and then pantomime (actions without words) various ways in which people steal, followed by acting out various ways in which to make amends for such stealing (as Zaccheus did when he gave back four times what he had taken from others).

Dealing with your students as individuals, allowing for individual activity, and at the same time planning group activity of a good variety means you must deal creatively with the space and equipment available to you. Most churches provide a room with a few chairs, or perhaps only a spare corner. You will often not have ideal facilities. But you can still do a lot with what you have. For one thing, you need not be confined to one room. There may be other places in the church to meet now and then. When the weather permits, a nearby park is a good substitute. Hospitals, old people's homes, private homes—all these can be effective meeting places, especially for older children. One teacher, for example, took her junior high age group to a nearby hotel where many old people lived. During the regular Sunday school hour, the students served tea and cookies to the people who lived there, talked with them, sang, and read the Bible. Many of the residents took part, delighted to have a little young company to break up the monotony of their otherwise dreary, lonely day. Afterwards, the class discussed the commandment "Honor thy father and mother." The teacher found the students very much moved by the experience, for they had learned an unforgettable lesson about the wisdom of God's command. They had seen the results of their society's neglect of the elderly. Many remarked that the children of those lonely old people would probably, and justly so, find themselves in the same sad situation some day!

Of course, you must also use the room given to you. You can make the most of it by having certain materials available to you. The following is a list that may serve as a guide: a blackboard, bulletin board, or wall space for hanging art displays; equipment for showing movies or slides; a box of clothes usable for costumes and some simple stage props for creative dramatics; a rug for sitting on the floor; a few small tables to allow for small group discussion or projects; art supplies such as clay, chalk, poster and water paints, crayons, pencils, various sorts of paper, glue, scissors, old magazines and newspapers, and a good supply of books and magazines to supplement the lesson material for older children (your church library should have such materials for you); a record player and records; a few simple musical rhythm instruments; and some song books.

Plan well which materials you want to use each time. Include a variety of materials that will allow you to teach the lesson, and allow the children to respond to it in different ways. There is a wise old saying that no one truly possesses a truth until he has shared it with someone else. Give your students an opportunity to do that!

To encourage your students to feel at ease, to share, to participate to the fullest extent, keep the feeling of the classroom informal. If you use chairs, avoid straight rows like church pews. Arrange them in a circle, a horseshoe, or two parts facing each other, or several small circles. Your students should be facing each other and you for the best communication. Don't forget the importance of involving your students through music, movement, art, discussion, and prayer. If they are old enough (eight and up) let them help plan and decide what to do at least some of the time. They may hesitate at first, make mistakes, and proceed slowly and awkwardly. But they will grow and learn by having to do more themselves than they would by your doing it.

Naturally, you are the one who decides what the subject material for a lesson is to be. Often your decision will be based on a teacher's manual or lesson plan outline provided by your church. You will, however, be prepared to alter that lesson plan if, during the sharing period with your students, you discover some need that can best be met with other material. In addition, the circumstances in which your students find themselves, and the things going on in all of your lives, can be a part of your lesson material. These things cannot be written down for you; you must see them for yourself. That is where creativity comes in. If there should be a major disaster, or some member of your church experiences a special joy or sorrow—these are things you should weave into the lesson material. In that way, every week your students will clearly experience the fact, through your teaching, that the faith they are learning about is part of every facet of their existence and relevant to all that is going on in and around them. Think of it this way: As a creative teacher, you must weave the two strands of God's revelation and His dealing in the events which shape our lives, into one unified whole. In this way your students will see the fact of God's providence in the past and present, on a large scale, and in the smallest details of their own lives, and feel that they are deeply rooted in and surrounded by His mysterious goodness and beauty, part of His loving plan to make them all worthy bearers of His image.

All of this is a rather difficult assignment. Creative teaching is a task requiring everything you can give it. But you need not do it alone. There are many people in your church and community who have special qualities of character, experience, and knowledge which you can use. Make a special point of building up a sort of resource list to use during the year. I well remember, for example, a time when a Sunday school teacher of mine was dealing with the text, "In Christ there is neither Jew nor Greek, bond nor free, male nor female." For that lesson, a black man from a neighboring church came to the class and told us how he felt united with all Christians of other races through Christ; and also what he thought still needed to be done to break down the barriers that existed between black and white, even in the church. That hit home a lot harder than the same words would have, coming from my white teacher. Another example was the time that a friend of mine had her husband, a doctor, come in and talk to her teen-age class about the effects of smoking, drinking, and drugs on the body. He was very objective and clinical, and there was no heavy-handed moralizing. He just gave them the plain facts. The lesson for that day was on the fact that we, as Christians, are not our own but belong to Christ, and that our bodies are His temples. The effect of that doctor's talk was memorable. The students sat entranced, hanging on every word. After the doctor was done, the teacher simply closed the class with silent prayer and a reading of the text. Afterwards, many parents called her to thank her for the positive effect the doctor's words had on their children at a time when they were facing a real crisis about such decisions. If there are any colleges in your town, don't be afraid to use the advice and presence of teachers in art, children's education, and Bible.

In conclusion, then, you as a creative teacher have a challenging and inspiring task. You are to guide your students' learning into the most important truths they will ever have to face. How you do that is of utmost importance. If it is at all possible, do not allow yourself to have more than ten to twelve students, since any number beyond that will inevitably dilute the effectiveness of your teaching. With a larger number, you won't know your students as well, nor will they be able to get as close to each other and become the kind of loving, close-knit group you are striving to create. You don't need expensive equipment or a fancy meeting space, but you do need to use your imagination to make the most of what you have, and to gather together a good variety of inexpensive materials to help students learn in the best possible way.

You will have all sorts of different subject matters to deal with. But above all, your subject matter must be Christ—the

Christ hidden in the Old Testament and revealed fully in the New Testament. But He must also be the living, present Christ who loves and is with you and each of your students. If you can help your students reach out a little bit to understand and receive that deep love of Christ, you will have done a great thing. Above all, keep your relationship with Him right. For unless your life is being lived in obedience to Him, and a constant communion in prayer in fellowship with other Christians and in your own private corner, no amount of work and technique will make up for the radiance of His presence in your life. It is His gift—the gift of His presence. But you must open yourself to Him and practice that presence, so that when you teach, you teach from your real life experience. Then your children will know that your teaching is not just words, but is wrung from an honest, personal struggle and a very real following after Christ. Then God can use your creative teaching to create within the children the new hearts and right spirits which He requires, and which are the true fulfillment and highest joy of every human being.

4 UNDERSTANDING OUR SUNDAY SCHOOL CHILDREN

Katie Gunnink

The supreme responsibility of the Sunday school teacher is the spiritual nurture of his pupils. Above all, he wants each of them to become a man of God thoroughly furnished unto all good works. To achieve this purpose of fostering spiritual growth, the teacher must understand the nature of the child. Jan Waterink once gave an illustration to show that even when we have our goals clearly established, our materials well organized, and our lesson planned, we can still fail in our purpose. There was a boy who decided to catch some fish for his mother to fry for supper. He had all his equipment ready. He also decided he wanted to take the fish home alive, so he had to have a container to put them in. He chose a paper bag. There was nothing wrong with his fishing equipment, nor with his carefully formed plans. His purpose was clear but he never got the fish home. His problem was that he didn't understand the nature of a paper bag. So too, humanly speaking, we as teachers can fail in our purpose when we fail to understand the nature of the child. In this article we will

Katie Gunnink, Grand Rapids, Michigan, is the head of the Christian Education department at the Reformed Bible College.

discuss four laws of development which we hope will give some guidelines in understanding our children.

The first law is the law of progressive growth. Briefly stated it is simply this: the child develops in successive stages from infancy to maturity, each stage marked by common characteristics and each stage an advance toward the fully mature person. The most beautiful example of this law is given to us in the Bible's characterization of the boyhood and youth of the Lord Jesus. In Luke 2:40 we read, "And the child grew, and waxed strong, filled with wisdom: and the grace of God was upon him." This text summarizes the childhood of Jesus in one brief sentence, "The child grew." Then it goes on to tell us that this growth was physical, mental, and spiritual. The growing of childhood is an automatic thing. A child doesn't self-consciously make himself grow. He just grows. There is something passive and receptive about a child's growing. He just takes in what is offered in his environment and assimilates it. He absorbs the spiritual atmosphere that surrounds him. He is part of the communal life of his family and community and catches its spirit, its values, and imitates its examples.

Luke 2:52 characterizes briefly the young manhood of Jesus: "And Jesus advanced in wisdom and stature, and in favor with God and men." Jesus' youth is briefly summarized in the words "Jesus advanced"; and then Scripture lists the dimensions in which this advancement took place: the mental, the spiritual, and the social. According to Young's *Concordance* the word *increase* or *advance* here means 'to strike forward." Notice that the word *advance* has a different meaning than the word *grow*, which characterized His childhood. One commentator explains the word *advance* in this way: "The word used here is derived from pioneers cutting down trees for the pathway of an advancing army." The idea is of one chopping a path for himself, beating his way onward, hacking a way in order to proceed. The word implies a deliberate, self-conscious, strenuous activity rather than passive, automatic development associated with the word *grow*. Adolescence is the path of volitional responsibility. The adolescent is still under the benevolent authority of his parents, but he feels responsible for his own decisions. He must achieve self-discipline and integration of his personality. He must make his own choices and establish his own philosophy of life. Note that this characterization of Jesus was given after His visit to the temple at age twelve, when He became conscious of His Messianic person and calling. In the temple the boy Jesus had made a self-conscious, deliberate choice. "Wist ye not that I must be about my Father's business?"

Scripture has thus characterized broadly two main cycles or stages of growth: that of childhood and adolescence. These two broad cycles are again broken down into subdivisions such as early, middle, and later childhood or adolescence.

How can we use this law of progressive growth in dealing with our Sunday school pupils? First, there is the concern for proper departmentalization. This is a problem in organization but it is an important aspect to consider. Children are conscious of peer groups. Even primaries don't like to be with the "little" children or to be called "little" children. They know they are quite advanced compared to kindergartners and preschoolers. Junior highs consider juniors "little kids." Every child feels his "grown-up-ness" and wants to be recognized and given responsibilities in keeping with his stage of development. Don't talk down to a child. Remember that childhood is the receptive stage. Children accept what you say for truth and they imitate their elders. Adolescents are not going to accept everything you say. They will question, test, argue, evaluate, and analyze critically. They are striking forward on their own. They need time to consider, to weigh, and to reach their own decisions. Be a wise, patient counselor and friend in these struggling years.

A second consideration in applying this law is that we must not be so conscious of group characteristics that we forget the individual. There are common characteristics to each stage of development, but these are general. One can expect a junior child to be a noisy, boisterous youngster, a baseball fan, and a tree-climbing Tarzan. But we may have a junior in our class that does not fit this characterization at all. He may be a reader preferring a book to a ball game. He may be quiet and studious. All adolescents are supposed to have problems, doubts, and struggles. But you may have an adolescent who is so self-disciplined and integrated that he adjusts without much difficulty to the stresses and strains of adolescence. Children want you to understand them as a group, but they also want you to know them as individual persons different from all the others. Know them by name, know about their hobbies, their pets, and their families. Accept them as individuals. Some are quick to learn, others slow. Plan to have a response from the slow ones that is in keeping with their ability and another kind of response from the brighter ones. One way to offend a child is to say, "Why can't you be like your brother, or like your friend Peter?" A child wants to be himself and be accepted for what he is—a person with his own abilities and his own growth pattern.

A third application of this law is a comfort and a warning. Growth is not an even, unvarying process. It takes place in spurts. This is important in evaluating a child's progress physically, mentally, socially, and spiritually. There will be "plateaus"—times when we can observe very little progress and thus become discouraged. We may feel we are doing very little for this child. He is not responding to our teaching. He is not growing. We look for changed lives as a result of our teaching, but this takes time and there are many ups and downs in the growth pattern. We experience it in our own lives. We are not always at a high peak spiritually; and we may expect with our children, too, that there will be times when spiritual growth seems at a standstill. Teachers, of all people, need patience. They can only evaluate from a long-range point of view. The important standard for evaluation is: What is the direction of the child's life? What is the poise of his soul, the bend of his heart?

A second law of growth is the law of sequence. Simply stated, it is that a child must learn to do certain things before he can do other things. Physically, he sits before he stands and stands before he walks. He uses large muscles before he uses small muscles. Mentally, he talks before he reads. Socially he learns to cooperate with one playmate before he can adjust to two or three. At five he is expected to relate to a whole group of kindergartners. John Calvin summarized spiritual sequence in growth when he wrote, "They [children] are renewed also by the Spirit of God according to the capacity of their age, 'till that power which was concealed within them grows by degrees and becomes fully manifest at the proper time.' "

In applying the law, we first consider the problem of readiness. What are the Biblical truths children are ready to receive? Small children understand what is concrete and tangible. The world of sense—of sound, touch, and smell—is a real and fascinating world. They are not ready for symbolism and abstract truths. They can appreciate God as creator, provider, protector, and a God who forgives. How can we determine a child's readiness? A few of the indexes are his questions, his behavior problems, his prayers, and his responses to our questions.

Two important aspects of sequence development involve the child's concept of God and of sin. A child's first response to God is that of reverence for God and His Word. He learns that God and the Bible are very special. God is thought of in anthropomorphic terms (human terms). He thinks of God in a physical way. God is high up in the sky. He is very old. God's attributes are meaningful in terms of his experiences with father and mother. Father and mother love him, accept him, and care for him. So God is like that. Mother and father are angry with him, punish him, and forgive him when he is sorry. God is like that. Mother's eyes are everywhere. Mother knows what her child is doing even when she can't see him. Mother is everywhere present. God is like that. Father knows everything and is strong enough to do anything. God is like that. Mother and father are dependable. They would never abandon him. God is like that. Children love the Lord Jesus because He is a kind, loving friend who loves children.

Juniors accept the fact of God. They also believe that Jesus came into the world to save them from sin. This faith is real, but it is naive. It is uncomplicated. It is accepted as a fact without question or doubt. God and Jesus are great heroes. The child glories in the power of God, the miracles of Jesus, and His wonderful victory over sin, the devil, death, and the grave.

The adolescent wants a real experience of Jesus as personal Savior. He wants to know Christ as a friend and guide.

The guilt feelings of a preschooler and primary child are in terms of an experience of estrangement. The child feels alienated when he does wrong or displeases his parents and teacher. He feels rejected. There is a distance between him and the people on whom his life and happiness depend. This is an intolerable feeling. This estrangement must be resolved. It is resolved by the child's sorrow and confession. Then there must be real forgiveness and an acceptance that makes the status as if the wrong had never been done. This lays the basis for the child's experience of God's forgiveness.

The junior child is a legalist. He thinks of sin in terms of outward acts. He is conscious of wrong acts and right acts, of bad people and good people. He does not yet appreciate the truth that his whole being is bad inside. The adolescent begins to feel real sin consciousness in the sense that he knows himself to be a sinner. His wrong thoughts come from within his own sinful heart. It is not just a matter of wrong acts, but of a wicked heart. God must not only forgive me; He must cleanse and renew my heart.

This law of sequence ought to lead us to consider seriously whether we are building upon previous stages of growth. Do we introduce new lessons in terms of what is already experienced and known? We have to ask, How much has this child experienced? How much does he understand? The law of sequence was summarized by Jesus in Mark 4:28, "First the blade, then the ear, then the full grain in the ear."

The third law of growth is that growth is organic. The child develops as a whole, not in parts. The physical, mental, social, and spiritual all develop together in a total growth process. Growth is not in isolated units but in relationship.

There is a relationship between the physical and the spiritual. The child brings his body with him to Sunday school (as every Sunday school teacher is well aware). His muscles are crying out for activity, his senses keen to hear, touch, see, smell, and handle. His muscles and his senses must be used to promote spiritual growth and understanding.

There is a relationship between the mind, the heart, and the will. Real learning involves the whole child. A child who looks with awe and wonder at God's beautiful creation is not only intellectually saying, "God made the sky, God made the flowers," but his whole person is involved in an act of worship. Therefore it is important to plan for a response that is not just testing for information but that is also concerned for attitudes, feelings, and Christian behavior.

The final law of growth is given us in Scripture. "Train up a child in the way he should go and when he is old he will not depart from it." God implants the seed of the new life, but it is our high calling as teachers to nurture the new life. A child becomes a growing Christian through the Word of God. God has promised that this nurture through His Word is effective in the spiritual development of His children. He has laid it down as a law: train a child in the good and right way and he will not depart from it. This is an awesome responsibility and an inestimable privilege. Every Christian teacher should have the ideal of Paul, "Teaching every man in all wisdom that we may present every man perfect in Christ."

5 SUNDAY SCHOOL—AN EVANGELISM ARM OF THE CHURCH

Henry Hoekstra

About seventy-five years ago a Sunday school teacher, in a little-known church southwest of Grand Rapids, taught a small class of nine- and ten-year-old girls the lesson for the week. Among the matters discussed was the teaching that all men were sinners through the fall and disobedience of Adam and Eve. The teacher, being led by the Holy Spirit, explained it in the following words: "We sin because we are sinners; we do not become sinners by sinning."

This statement is not so profound that everybody should take note, but one of the girls did take it to heart and pondered on it. She remembered the statement and somehow it never left her.

About sixty years later this girl started attending a chapel, and after some time confessed Jesus Christ as her Savior. During the instruction period a discussion was held on the subject of man being born a sinner. This woman, after some sixty years of not attending church, remembered the lesson

Henry Hoekstra, Allegan, Michigan, is the missionary pastor at the Christian Reformed church and former member of the denominational Sunday School Committee.

she learned in Sunday school. She recalled "man sins because he is a sinner; he does not become a sinner by sinning." Certainly the Sunday school can be an arm of evangelism of the church!

The Sunday school is related to the church just as the arm is related to the human body. It is part of the body itself. The leaders of the Sunday school must take into consideration that it is not the church, but one facet of the church.

However, the church, as an organization, must recognize the Sunday school to be what she is—an arm, truly a part of the body of Christ. It must be stated that it is possible to overemphasize the Sunday school just as it is possible to underrate its importance.

In order to keep the Sunday school in its correct perspective it should be directly responsible to and supported by the official church board. A Sunday school operating without this close relationship with the official board would be like a physical arm attempting work without the human body. And let's remember that a body without an arm is greatly handicapped.

The arm of evangelism, ideally speaking, should be made up of the entire congregation of believers. Parents can be a powerful example to their children in considering the Sunday school as an agency to reach the people in the community of the church.

The pastor or educational director can promote the Sunday school by showing public appreciation to the teachers and students who play an active role in the Sunday school program. He should alert the whole congregation to the challenge of gathering in "the other sheep and lambs" and creating a church team spirit.

In recruiting teachers and helpers the director can learn from the method Jesus used to enlist the seventy in Luke 10: 1-16. Jesus clearly explained their responsibilities, the sacrifices they would be called on to make, what procedures they were to follow, and the kind of responses they could expect. Imagine that scene when Jesus personally, warmly, and carefully enlisted the seventy. The workers responded by being obedient and anticipating the work of the Holy Spirit in and through their lives. These seventy came back with joy (Luke 10:17a)! They were glad because they had experienced spiritual victories and they knew Jesus was working through them.

Those involved in the Sunday school program of the present-day church also experience the same joy. They can be used to bring in those who have not as yet been reached effectively for the Lord. With His blessing they can see the power of the gospel working in the lives of the "other sheep and lambs" and miraculously bring them to salvation and lead them to spiritual maturity. God often uses the team spirit of the church which sees the challenge in reaching the people in their community for Christ.

The Sunday school is an evangelism arm when it directly carries out the proclamation of the evangel. Only when its superintendent, secretary, teachers, and all who assist are dedicated to Christ and His church is it an arm of the body. The staff of workers is easily the most important tool in the arm of the church.

These Sunday school teachers should be carefully selected out of the body for their being living members—truly born again men and women who know God's Word and are filled with the Holy Spirit. They ought to be men and women who are aware of why God, in His grace, has saved them. They know that God has saved them to serve Him in feeding and caring for the flock and also that part of the flock Jesus refers to in John 10:16: "And other sheep I have, which are not of this fold: them also I must bring, and they shall hear my voice; and they shall become one flock, one shepherd."

These teachers should be encouraged to learn the principles of leading a soul to Christ. They should be encouraged to attend the Sunday school and evangelism conferences.

The church should make a concerted effort to provide the teacher with the best available equipment, including classrooms, blackboards, visual aids, and busses that are operated by drivers who love God. They should have Biblically oriented Sunday school material prepared by those who know how to reach the unchurched child and adult. It should be noted that in our day of changing values and techniques it is necessary to evaluate the lesson material at least once a year.

The music which is used in a Sunday school where community children are attending should be simple and evangelistic. Simple Scriptural songs and choruses should be taught. Copies of the words should be given to children to take home for their parents to teach them the words. Inexpensive song books can be given to students as gifts.

In order for the Sunday school to be an effective arm in evangelism for the church, it should be aware of those who live in their community, as well as those who are moving into their area. In order to do this the entire church should be recruited to make a survey, and then by the block captain system continue to observe the "other sheep," seeking always to bring them into the fold.

A community type bulletin could be of great value to make the community aware of the church and Sunday school.

The Sunday school students can often bring their unchurched friends and neighbors. A membership drive or contest boosts the rolls and gives the present members an opportunity to participate in the outreach as well. The daily vacation Bible school students are good prospects for Sunday school growth.

Other means which can be used to make the community aware of your church are entering floats in parades, advertising in local papers, backyard Bible classes, and special programs.

The attention should not only be focused on children, but young people and adults too should be visited and brought in. Ideally, the entire family should attend Sunday school if it is to be a successful arm of evangelism. If our church members would set the example by attending Sunday school as a family, the community families would be more apt to do so too.

It is a proven fact that what a family will do together will tend to be more meaningful to them. This has a good effect on the parent-children relationship as well. When only part of the family comes under the influence of the gospel an added strain is experienced. Younger children often become confused and frustrated when the Sunday school teacher faithfully emphasizes the importance of having Christ in their lives and yet father or mother claim they can get along quite well without Christ.

In having the entire family attend Sunday school there would also be the possibility of having family discussion of the lessons they had in their respective classes. Then, too, the parents would be exposed to other members of the church. The results of such Sunday school strategy is obvious—it would indeed result in "the arm" being used to bring entire families instead of only individuals into the fold.

The Sunday school is often preferred above the regular church service by those seeking to know Christ because they have the opportunity to ask questions in the class. It can also be used as a stepping-stone to the church service, since Sunday school attendance by young people and adults takes away some of the fear they have of attending church services.

It is also the experience of many churches that rarely does a child come to a full surrender to Christ when the parents have no contact with the church. One experiences that it is relatively simple to get children of the community to attend Sunday school, and every effort should be made to do so. These children can be a means by which the parents and their older brothers and sisters can be reached as well.

The Sunday school as an arm of the body of Christ cannot overlook the needs of the restless young people of the community. The young people of our day show a tremendous interest in knowing what God says in His Word. Billy Graham often says that the young people are screaming for attention. The Sunday school should attend to that need which they are indicating by their actions.

Finally, we call all members of the body of Christ to the most effective tool of all—prayer. Let the teachers be in prayer for the individual students, naming them daily in intercessory prayer; but the needs of the Sunday school are a proper cause for everyone in the congregation to remember before the the throne of grace.

We often experience having new members come for a short time and then apparently lose interest and stay away. Here are some workable suggestions that may avoid this problem.

1. The entire Sunday school should be oriented to the concept of accepting newcomers and making them feel that they are welcome. The teacher can be an effective example in this matter.

2. The teacher should show an interest in these visitors and indicate to the class that he is genuinely happy the new student has come.

3. The teacher can use some method of recognizing the new student's presence. The type of recognition should be chosen according to the age of the student.

4. Special events, outings, and picnics can stimulate interest.

5. Home visits by the Sunday school teachers are helpful, particularly in those homes where the parents do not attend church or Sunday school.

6. Parent-teacher meetings can help to give the parents an appreciation of the teacher's efforts.

7. Occasional notes, letters, or phone calls to the homes will inform parents of achievements and activities of the class.

8. Remember the students' birthdays and other special occasions with a card, and give them public recognition in Sunday school.

9. Give students ample opportunity to express themselves in class.

10. Use any of the talents the new students may have.

11. Teachers should observe any need the student may have (clothing, food, etc.).

A very important facet of a successful Sunday school is its records kept on the students. These are some of the records that should be kept:

1. Enrollment records. In comparing this record with the attendance record, one can know the extent of absenteeism.

2. Attendance records. These are necessary to indicate growth or decline. (Rewards for good attendance can help stimulate regularity in attendance.)

3. Absentee records. Careful follow-up work should be carried out to analyze the causes for absenteeism. Removal from records should be considered for only these reasons:

a. The pupil moves away.
b. The pupil dies.
c. The pupil regularly attends another Sunday school.
d. The pupil requests to have his name removed.

4. Prospects records. This perhaps can be gleaned from a community survey or from records of new neighbors. Encourage everyone in your Sunday school to look for new prospects. Included in this record should be those who graduate from the nursery rolls.

5. Visitors records. Use your church guest register for this. Any visitors who sign the register and indicate they have no church home should be followed up.

Can we expect results from the Sunday school which seeks to be an arm of evangelism in the church? History will prove to an observing person that the church with such an arm is a living church and certainly a growing church. The efforts are well rewarded. Generally there will be those who will come to confess Jesus Christ as their Lord and Savior.

Even if this would not be the result, the Christian cannot afford to neglect these precious ones in his community. The command of the Lord is sufficient reason for our careful and prayerful efforts of reaching the other sheep. The faithful efforts of the teacher may not show immediate results; but, like the nine-year-old-girl who sixty years later remembered what the teacher had said, those efforts will be rewarded some day, in some way, by our Lord. Hospital chaplains, doctors, nurses, and pastors can all testify of deathbed statements of elderly people, who give testimony of knowing something of sin, forgiveness, and heaven because a faithful teacher taught the evangel in a Sunday school. Even though a faithful teacher does urge and press the student for a decision for Christ, he is not commanded to convert them. His task is to deliver the message from God's Word according to His will. "God giveth the increase." We can claim the promise of God: "My word ... shall not return unto me void, but it shall accomplish that which I please, and it shall prosper in the thing whereto I sent it" (Isa. 55:11).

God has used this arm of evangelism in the past, He is using it today, and He will continue to use it until Christ returns. Those who are active in holding up this arm in sincere efforts and prayer can be assured of hearing Him say, "Well done, thou good and faithful servant."

The Sunday school is a result of the religious revival of the eighteenth century. The love of God, felt with new power through the preaching of the revival, stirred men to love and serve the Lord. The first Sunday school was opened in 1780 by Robert Raikes of Gloucester, England. It was through this new movement that children, who ordinarily were not reached, came to hear the Gospel truth.

The Sunday school in our day has a great challenge. For every one thousand unreached children and adults of 1780 there are millions today.

May this strong arm of the church now experience another revival and reach out as never before and by the grace of God be used to bring in the lost sheep that are His "other sheep" and gather them in His fold.

6 THE SUNDAY SCHOOL SUPERINTENDENT

Wendell J. Schaal

Who is the first one to get it in the neck if your favorite baseball team is doing poorly? Nine chances out of ten it will be the manager. The manager is expected to produce, and the team reflects his attitudes and way of doing things. If he does an excellent job and his team is a winner he'll probably be named manager of the year. If the team has a poor record he will most likely be invited to use his talents elsewhere. So too with the Sunday school superintendent. The Sunday school will be as good or poor as the superintendent himself.

Sometimes the Sunday school is in trouble before the year even starts. Why? Due to the process by which a superintendent is either elected or appointed. You know how it can go. We look around and say, "Well, let's see, who hasn't been stuck with the job yet?" Sound familiar? This is rather a hit-and-miss approach, not guaranteed to get the best person possible. Therefore, it is imperative that the proper selection process be used to obtain the best qualified person.

Wendell J. Schaal, Grand Rapids, Michigan, is the superintendent of the Sunday school, Boston Square Christian Reformed Church in Grand Rapids, Michigan, and a former teacher.

What makes a good candidate for superintendent? He will possess many qualities and be many things. He will be a dedicated Christian, filled with the Spirit and with a sincere love for children. He will be prayerful, Bible reading, and willing to devote his time and efforts to the job. He will either have demonstrated proven administrative and management talent or show ability to run the organization. He must have the full support of the staff and consistory.

Once the Sunday school has such a person—hang on to him! He is a valuable person indeed. And a word of advice to the superintendent: make that your full-time church job. Don't spread yourself thin by being involved in a lot of other things. The Sunday school will suffer as a result.

At this point, let's look at what the superintendent's energies are used for:

1. Securing a competent teaching staff which should have the same dedication as the superintendent. A sometimes forgotten member of the staff is an energetic and enthusiastic song leader who can also bring in outside musical talent.
2. Selecting proper lesson materials.
3. Organizing the Sunday school into departments.
4. Arranging teachers' meetings.
5. Setting the time for Sunday school.
6. Securing proper facilities.
7. Arranging for programs of special interest to the Sunday school.
8. Considering the value of collection, purpose, and disbursement of funds.
9. Making special awards for attendance, class achievement, and memory work.
10. Outlining the functions of each officer.
11. Presenting aims and goals to the teaching staff.
12. Maintaining proper discipline.
13. Keeping the lines of communications open between the staff and the consistory. Remember, you need their support too, especially if you contemplate making changes.

Now let's backtrack and elaborate on the above items. Your staff makes the whole program go, just as the players make the ball team operate. Therefore it is vitally important that you have the best people possible. They must be equally as dedicated to their task as you are to yours. Communicate with your staff. Know their needs as a group and individually. Make them well aware of your appreciation of their time and efforts, and whenever possible speak positively to them.

There are two directions to go in lesson materials—the single lesson based on the same Bible text or the graded material based on different texts and geared to the various age levels of the children. With the uniform lesson you can have teachers' meetings of the whole staff and the same lesson plans can be followed. With the graded material, teachers' meetings of the whole are impossible except for business meetings. You have to meet by department, which may run as high as five different groupings. This may necessitate combining with various churches and having corresponding departments meet together. You should be well aware of the ramifications involved before deciding which material to use. The important thing is that Jesus Christ is thymain theme.

Sunday school organization is tied in with materials used. If you use the single lesson concept you can have a primary and secondary department. If you use graded materials you have to organize along the lines of materials used, which will most likely involve five different departments: preschool and kindergarten, grades one and two, three and four, five and six, and seven and eight.

No matter how you are organized you must have teachers' meetings involving your entire staff at least once a month. You have to keep the lines of communication open between the teachers and yourself and among the various teachers with each other. This is necessary to maintain a high degree of enthusiasm and devotion in the staff.

What is the best time for Sunday school to meet? It may not necessarily be after the Sunday morning worship service. After sitting in church for up to one and a half hours, the children can be fidgety and may not be so ready to settle down in Sunday school. Consider having Sunday school meet prior to the morning service—for example, at 9:30, with church meeting at 11:00. Here is an instance where you need the cooperation of the entire consistory. (Remember those lines of communication?)

Proper facilities are important. Ideally each class should have its own room equipped with tables and chairs, blackboards, chalk, erasers, posterboards, Bibles, and flannelgraphs. You need the right tools to get the job done.

You should have special programs periodically, if for no other reason than a change of pace. It may be a missionary program, it may be a movie, or it may be all special music; the important thing is to have them.

Select special causes for various collections. Let the children know ahead of time what the collection is to be used for. Advertise it, sell it, and you'll be surprised how well the children give. Set a dollar amount and break it down to so much per child. They will come through. Just ask some parents about how they are "bugged" by their child for that special project.

Any child loves to be told what a great job he has done, especially in front of his peers. So reward him for attendance, memory work, or a special contribution. The next thing you know some other kids will want a reward also. Set the goals for them and watch them strive for it. Enthusiasm is contagious!

Delegate duties whenever possible. This is what your officers are for. Each officer can take charge of a specific task or project. They are then more than mere figureheads. They will appreciate your confidence in them and help take a load off your shoulders.

It is your responsibility to set the tone for the year. This includes aim and goals. The staff has to know what these are, and they must believe in them personally. Some of the goals should be, making the children more aware of God, His way of salvation, and how to better love and serve Him. Make the children aware they are sinners and only through Jesus Christ can they be saved. Get them to use the Bible as a living guide for life. Strive to have them be a witness in the community. Grow in Christian love and character. Use the Sunday school as the best means possible for Christian instruction in the church.

Discipline must be inherent in any organization in that it is necessary to function properly. It should always be positive, constructive, and used with a definite purpose in mind. The word *punishment* should not be confused with discipline. Punishment is a form of discipline, but discipline is not automatically punishment. Discipline includes such things as one hundred percent attendance, punctuality, respectfulness, doing the work such as learning texts or completing exercises. Discipline applies to both teachers and pupils. Punishment is necessary when there is an infraction of the rules. Even here it should be kept positive. A child should know why punishment is being used and corrective measures are expected to be taken. It should be administered fairly, be proper for the infraction of rules, and not too harsh for the occasion.

Keeping the lines of communication open is very important. You need the back-up support and encouragement of your consistory. You need their interest and prayers. Consistory members should be invited and encouraged to visit the Sunday school in action, to see for themselves what your program goals are. You may even want to invite them to staff meetings at times to get the feelings of the teachers on various matters. This is especially true if you contemplate any changes from the established routine. You need their support, and without it you may find yourself having a hard job making such changes. At minimum, keep them informed of what you are doing.

The Sunday school is in essence a vital member of the church body, charged with the task of strengthening the children in the knowledge of and commitment to Christ, and—just as important—gathering new members into the flock.

There are some definite steps a superintendent can take to build up the Sunday school numerically. The first thing that must be done is to study your community. To put it in sales terms: What is your market potential? Canvass your area and discover how many children are out there that are not attending any Sunday school. Now you know how many you could possibly have in Sunday school. The next step is to enlist workers to go out and invite—or recruit, if you please—

prospects to your Sunday school. For every worker you have, you are bound to get several new members. Next, make sure you have ample physical space for your new recruits. You can't enlarge the Sunday school if you don't have room for the children. Once you have them there, you must be sure you have competent and trained teachers. The Lord used trained disciples to spread the gospel and so should you. Now keep building; use your new students to bring friends. Once a class builds up to ten, split the class and build them back up. In other words, divide and multiply. In conclusion, here are ten basics especially applicable for an evangelistic Sunday school, but also true for children of your own church.

1. Make the Bible the center and core of your study.
2. Define your aims and objectives.
3. Secure spiritually dedicated, doctrinally grounded, pedagogically trained, and sacrificially enthusiastic teachers.
4. Adapt your program and methods to the needs of your community.
5. Condition the church to a Sunday school that is in fact and deed an evangelistic arm of the church.
6. Institute an effective recruitment program.
7. Strive to win your pupils to Christ, the church, and a life of Christian service.
8. Know your pupils' individual needs, backgrounds, problems, and interests in order to work effectively with them.
9. Learn by doing. (Arise and go! Acts 8:26.)
10. Pray without ceasing (I Thess. 5:17).

7 THE SUNDAY SCHOOL TEACHER— A LOOK AT YOURSELF

John H. Schaal

Have you ever sat down for a few moments and taken a look at yourself? Surely you have seen yourself in the mirror hundreds of times, but this is a different kind of look. Look at yourself in several ways: how God made you—in His image with many gifts and assets which, in Christ, make you to be like Him; how you have grown and developed through the years physically, mentally, and spiritually; and how you are as a person, teacher, and leader right now. You will see many things about yourself and in yourself that cause you to thank God for making you as He did. You may see some aspects about yourself that are unpleasant, but thank God for giving you the opportunity to better yourself as a result of this inspection. Among other aspects of yourself that you will notice, take a view and a study of the obvious ones and the ones that may need some improving if you are to be a good teacher. You may call these things the teacher's God-given tools.

The voice and speaking

If you are to communicate the truths of the gospel to others—and you are called to be Christ's witness according to

Acts 1:8—one of the most important tools that God has given you is your voice. Many people are not really acquainted with their voice, for most are shockingly surprised at the sound and impression of their voice as recorded on tape.

For a time be conscious of your voice, your speaking, and the way it affects the people with whom you deal. Try to develop your voice so that you speak in the lower register—softly and yet plainly enough so that everyone will hear. The ideal projection of the voice is to speak so that the student will eagerly pay attention and yet not have to strain in order to hear you. One teacher was most effective with fifth graders. She spoke very softly yet clearly. In discovering the secret of her success she stated that she had had a voice problem and therefore had to conserve her strength on the order of a doctor who told her not to speak loudly or any more than necessary. At that time she learned the lesson of proper voice control and use. Try that prescription yourself and see how it works.

Another rule for improving your voice is to cultivate and work on the use of the vowels: *a, e, i, o, u*. Sound them in the lower register and then gradually work up to a higher pitch and hear the difference. Exaggerate the use of your lips, tongue, and jaw, observing how you respond so that you will continue to make better use of them. Open your mouth wide when you speak so that you will speak distinctly; in fact, try speaking superdistinctly to see the effect you create. Of course, these exercises are not intended to be practiced on your students, but are to be done either alone or with another person who is interested in improving his teaching ability. Try either saying or singing the vowels listed above, holding the notes for a considerable time.

Your voice gives a clue to your personality; therefore, make it melodious, pleasant, and sufficiently effective. Do not shout unless you are dramatizing a point. By overuse of the voice or speaking loudly or too emphatically, you lose your effectiveness when you want to be emphatic and dramatic by loud sounds and overtones. Bear in mind these three words: pause—modulate—emphasize.

Your speech evaluated

Someday take this along to your class or to another place where you are speaking and have an assistant (if you have such in your class) or a friend check these items. If you are alone, immediately after a teaching session try to evaluate your work by checking over the following list:

An evaluation of your speech	*1	2	3	4	5
Delivery					
Directness					
Physical behavior					
Vocal variety					
Intelligibility					
Pronunciation					
Enthusiasm					
Pupil response					
Organization and lesson content					
Attention held					
Lesson presentation					
Statement of the primary goal					
Use of materials such as Bible, printed material, and visual aids					
Relevancy					
Seen easily					
Displayed only when used					
Simple and clear					
Prepared prior to use					
Use of motivation					
Satisfaction step					
Statement of the goal to be achieved					
Explanation of how it can be achieved					
Practical proof of achievement					
Application to life today					
Final overall evaluation of your objectives and goals achieved					

*1, poor; 2, fair; 3, average; 4, good; 5, excellent

Suggestions for improvement

Before you speak

Have a purpose, or goal, in mind.
Choose a subject that's interesting, challenging, entertaining, and timely.
Have a plan, and set a time limit.
Understand your audience and adjust your material to it.
Use many illustrations, stories, quotations, and similar interest-arousing devices.
Pay careful attention to your beginning and your ending.
Use repetition and restatement to emphasize main points and important ideas.

When you speak

Be poised, neatly dressed, and confident.
Speak with vigor and enthusiasm.
Keep eye contact with your listeners.
Let your posture and movement be dignified and easy, your gestures spontaneous.
Use language that is simple, colorful, and correct.
Enunciate clearly and pronounce correctly.
Vary your rate, pitch, volume, inflection, and pauses to avoid monotony.
Cultivate a warm, friendly, sincere manner.
Keep notes on small cards or not at all.
Observe the time limits you have set.

Where can I find material?

1. Think
2. Observe
3. Talk
4. Experience
5. Read

Your hands

When is the last time you held your hands up and took a long, good look at them? What for? To see if they were clean, to discover whether there was any sign of arthritis? No—rather to look at them as a wonderful masterpiece of creation to be used in ways that God intends. One of the most delicate creations of the body is the hand. As one medical student said shortly after he had studied the human hand: "It's a marvel to me that when I fling out my hands that all my fingers don't fly off into space." God indeed has made the hands a masterpiece of His workmanship, and you should use them correctly in your teaching. As you gesture with them, act out thoughts with them, and express various emotions by using them, you have an interesting teaching tool at your disposal.

One teacher taught with his arm bent at the elbow placed behind his back. His boy pupils nicknamed him the one-armed bandit because of that pose which became a part of his appearance. Another had the habit of spreading his fingers and with arms bent at the elbow placed his fingers together pressing them as an outlet for his nervousness at first and then later as a habit.

"What am I going to do with my hands?" For the moment be very conscious of them and then forget them; use them naturally to the best advantage by permitting them to be at your side or folded or used in gestures, being no more conscious of them than of the rest of your body when you are teaching.

Your hands, like your eyes, also speak a language—a universal language. With this language you call; you point the way; you express joy, victory, disgust, and even despair. The use of hands in gesturing is sometimes more effective than words. Winston Churchill made famous the sign of victory when he raised his hands and with two fingers forming a V, gestured to the crowds throughout the British Empire his faith in the final triumph of the Allies during World War II. No words could have expressed that faith so eloquently.

Your eyes and your face

Your eyes and face are the mirror to your soul. One of the reasons hippies used to wear dark glasses was to hide the soul from those with whom they had no fellowship or rapport.

Others can detect your moods and feelings even more quickly than you realize as they watch your whole bearing, especially your face and eyes. Remember, it takes more muscles to frown than it does to smile, and you must not be a person who needs a pin on your lapel to remind others that there are many reasons for smiling. The Christian, above all, needs to take to heart the expression of Philippians which states, "Rejoice . . . again I will say, Rejoice." A Sunday school teacher needs to breathe and show an inner radiance which comes out through the eyes and face as well as through our daily living. The eyes and face are good tools in maintaining discipline. If you are the right kind of teacher, you will use your face in teaching, in expressing radiance, optimism, hope, and the upward look. But you can also with flashing, blazing eyes express anger or disgust, and with set and determined eyes and face bring out a resolute purpose of carrying out the idea you wish to convey.

The three "H" tools

Your Heart—Teach with your heart aflame. That is to say, your whole personality must be thrown into your teaching.

Your Head—Teach with your head clear. That means proper study and not having your thoughts cluttered with the extraneous and worrisome ideas that Satan will try to thrust into your mind to keep you from being fully used by the Lord. It also means physical care such as exercise, diet, and rest. Your leisure hours, particularly the hours before you teach, are needed for meditation and not riotous celebration; for consecration and not dissipation.

Your Hands—Teach with your hands surrendered. "Take my hands and let them move, At the impulse of Thy love."

Your education

One of the severe handicaps you may face is the fact that you feel inferior as a teacher, but that need not be the roadblock that keeps you from service. Be thankful for the education you have and do not bemoan the lack of it. Even if five or ten years ago you were a dropout, that need not be a hindrance now for your Sunday school work. If you have caught the vision of wanting to be an effective worker in this branch of God's kingdom, begin picking up where you left off and start a new program of training. By getting help and training, eventually you will become so absorbed in the work that you will continue satisfying your thirst for knowledge and you will overcome the lack of it. Today there are many adult education programs available; and you are not so isolated that you cannot obtain help through correspondence courses, from your pastor who is always eager to see his flock improve, from the church library, which will have or obtain books that can be of help to you, from workshop training courses, and above all, from the high schools and colleges in your area. If you have the basic spiritual, mental, physical, and educational requirements to be a teacher, along with the spirit of dedication and consecration, your on-the-job training and teaching will give you ample opportunity to put the things you are studying from books, at evening courses, at workshops, and by correspondence into practice in the classroom situation. Remember, you will never be able to swim by completing a correspondence course. You need actual contact and experience in the water. So too, you will never become an effective teacher by taking all the courses offered even on a university level until you put into practice the things you have learned and until you put to use the talents and techniques in an actual classroom leadership situation.

Books are essential. The first requirement is a good Bible—one that has some lesson or cross-reference helps. You should not hesitate to mark your Bible with colored pencil as well as write ideas and thoughts in its margin. Use this in your teaching at every possible point.

Be prepared to purchase other books, lesson helps, and visual aid materials. Place books and other materials in your budget, and when gift days come along, such as Christmas and birthdays, let it be known that if you are to be remembered with a gift, these would be appreciated.

In using books, first page through all the chapters, then read with concentration the opening words, preface, and introduction. There the author states his approach to the subject and the goals he hopes you will achieve. After reading and reflecting on an entire chapter, read it again, this time underlining or indicating by side marks the paragraphs you wish to return to at some future time. For maximum value, you should keep the main ideas of the chapter in mind by outlining the trend of thought in the margin.

A Sunday school teacher should not begin his work until he has a Bible dictionary, a few books on methods of teaching, and lesson quarterlies, in addition to a workable Bible. As you build your library, obtain books of specific interest such as a Bible atlas, a one- or two-volume Bible commentary, and commentaries on individual Bible books. Each year books on the year's curriculum are published, together with lesson helps and commentary; these are a must for you.

Your dress

This is a day of informality, and it seems that in some circles you identify by dressing as your peers dress. This is not necessarily the rule to follow. Rather, if there is any blanket statement that must be made, it is that you should dress discreetly and neatly. In the classroom, the teacher should not be dressed gaudily and with a great deal of ornamentation, as this detracts from the message. Your aim should be that your dress and conduct will be inconspicuous and attractive, so that the message will be predominant. When you teach in Sunday school you are God's prophet and you represent Christ the King; therefore, dress well but not to the point of exaggeration, whether it be overdressed or shabbily dressed.

Your treasure chest—do you have one?

Begin thinking in terms of obtaining a treasure chest. It may be a notebook or two in which you store ideas, pictures, poems, quotations, articles, and other items that will be of assistance to you in teaching.

Your treasure chest may be a filing system into which,

under a variety of titles and headings, you place many items of value. Some have a set of shoe boxes, labeling the front of the box with subject titles. Such a treasure chest is unique and will be of particular help to you because you alone have assembled the material which fits your thinking and situation.

Conclusion

To the above practical hints you may add ideas of your own. Place a loose-leaf sheet at the end of this chapter, and when you attend a workshop, a Sunday school convention, or an extension class, take notes. When you get an inspiration or idea, jot it down.

As often happens when you read a book like this one, you may be more convinced of your inadequacy to fill the task to which you are called. This is not entirely undesirable, for it should lead you to several courses of action. We will call attention to two of them.

First, you should be more earnest in prayer. In this connection James 1:5, 6 will be of help to you: "But if any of you lacketh wisdom, let him ask of God, who giveth to all liberally and upbraideth not; and it shall be given him. But let him ask in faith, nothing doubting."

In addition, you will do some intensive looking at yourself—and that is what this chapter is all about—to see how you come out in the inventory. From this inventory, you will discover weak spots and areas that need improving. Being conscious of the needed changes, you will set about doing something about them. God has given you many blessings and talents that need cultivating and developing. That is the purpose of this chapter and this entire book—that you become a better servant for Him.

 PRESCHOOLERS—MINIATURE ADULTS?

Eileen Van't Kerkhoff

The Sunday school is the first group experience for most children. This is an important step for them. What are these children like that are coming to you?

Few people would describe preschool children as being "miniature adults," but when the Sunday school hour is planned for them, the same format—an opening followed by a Bible lesson— is used as for older children and adults. The ages of three, four, and five are very special years and these children have very special needs. Teachers recognize that their attention span is short and that these little ones are unable to sit still for long.

The three-year-old is interested in people, things, and ideas. He is growing up and is usually ready for a group setting, but sometimes he still acts like a toddler. But he will enjoy a cheerful, relaxing day with you. Know and accept

---

Eileen Van't Kerkhoff, Grand Rapids, Michigan, is a director of the Aldersgate preschool nursery. She has served as an elementary school teacher and has been active in Sunday school and daily vacation Bible school.

him for being three and try not to mold him into being an older child.

The four-year-old is busy, active, and noisy. He really wants to be part of a group. Sometimes he is very self-confident, and at other times he is easily crushed because someone ignored him or failed to praise his project.

The five-year-old is a slightly older, more mature version of the delightful three-year-old. He is more serene than when he was four. He is comfortably aware of who he is. He likes companionship and is very interested in a variety of things. He observes you and wants to do what you do. He can distinguish truth from fantasy.

So you are the teacher! Good teachers for preschoolers come in all sizes, ages, and educational backgrounds. They all share a genuine affection for children and an understanding of how young children think, feel, and act.

The teacher sets limits in her room with kindness and firmness. She knows that the best way to calm an upset, excited, angry, or fearful child is to remain very calm herself. She has the group under control.

How many teachers are needed? A ratio of one adult to every five children is preferable. With ten children there should be one teacher and one helper. It is best to keep the group small when possible. The size will also depend on the space available.

Children between the ages of three and five are different in many important ways from school-age children, and they need a different type of Sunday school. They cannot think in the abstract; they need a picture or some other type of visual aid. Their language is very imaginative, and discussion is usually not too helpful because they are interested only in what they say and not in listening to others. Their emotions are unstable; therefore they become upset easily and may find it hard to leave the security of the group to join a larger group for the Sunday school opening. Their physical coordination is still very limited. The teacher cannot expect too much from them in putting things together that are included in some Sunday school handiwork packets. Far too often it is the teacher's handiwork that completes the project.

Everyone wants these children to learn in the Sunday school. But they must learn physically, socially, and emotionally as well as intellectually, so that what they learn becomes a part of their total personality during these most formative years.

In view of these facts, which Sunday school program will provide this necessary balance of active and quiet times, to allow for both listening and doing? A well-planned program will prevent preschoolers from becoming unduly fatigued from too much passive sitting. This program should include:

10:00 Greeting by teacher, name tags,
prayer, songs,
Table activities

10:15 Storytime—Bible verse with puppet
Teach Bible story with various presentations

10:30 Special Activity time—an art expression of the Bible story
Light snack

10:45 Singing time, fingerplays or
flannelgraph story

The time for each activity must be flexible, so you can flow easily from one activity into another. During one Sunday session the storytime may be longer, or at another session the activity time may take just a few minutes and you can spend more time singing. Some days you might not have time for your flannelgraph or visual aid story. Let us consider each of these activities step by step:

Greeting by the teacher. The teacher greets the children at the door, seated on a chair so she is at the height of the children and on their eye level as she talks to them. She pins a name tag on the child to wear during the morning. The name tag should be made of stiff paper or felt and can be shaped like an apple, a leaf, or other simple design. It should be fastened by a safety pin or rolled piece of masking tape. Later in the year the teacher may use an attendance board;

for example, a flannelboard with colored sky, grass, trees, and little lambs with the children's names in a box below. The children put their lamb on the board to show they are present. This type of greeting gives a child a real sense of identity and belonging.

Prayer. Because the meeting place is God's house and children are dealing with spiritual truth, prayer should always mark the opening of the class session. Pray in language the child can understand and with thought concepts that deal with the immediate situation. Keep your prayers brief.

Singing. You may want to introduce a song or two at this point to get the class into a unified, joyous mood before entering any other activity. Or you may want to keep the singing in reserve for a later hour. However, if one or two songs are used now and then repeated later, the songs will be more easily retained.

After this the child is free to go to the table and work on activities set out by the teacher's helper. The helper is at the table to supervise, encourage, and help a child when necessary. Good table activities are puzzles (preferably wooden), which can be religiously oriented, books, and other manipulative things for young children. If the children have come from the church service or nursery where they were not served a snack, this is a good time to give them a cracker or "M and Ms." If the Sunday school session is held in the same room used for nursery, the table activities should be different from those available at the other part of the morning.

Storytime. This is the time to put away the table activities and sit on the rug for the Bible story. To arouse the preschoolers' eagerness for this time, use a simple hand puppet. My puppet is named Ko-Ko and storytime becomes Ko-Ko time. After the children are seated on the rug, I tell them I have a little friend in this little house, and if they call softly, "Ko-Ko," she will come out. They call her and she pops out and says "hi." Ko-Ko greets the children and introduces newcomers and visitors. Some days she calls the roll to see if all the children are present.

Ko-Ko teaches the Bible verse to the children. They can say the verse to her as she calls their names. Sometimes she says, "I know a new song today," and she sings it and teaches it to them.

Many children who are reluctant to speak when in a group, will talk to a puppet. They are very intrigued by a puppet and it becomes a real friend to them.

Any simple, attractive puppet purchased in a store can be used, or you can make a simple sock puppet like mine, which has yarn hair, buttons for eyes, and a red velvet mouth. One secret is to give the puppet a mouth that you can move as you talk and something floppy like yarn hair that will attract attention. A house for the puppet can be made from a paper box, cutting a window for the puppet to come out. Make a peak for the roof, paint the house with tempera paint, and decorate the front with flowers.

When you use the puppet, your helper can do the puppet and the puppet voice. If you are alone, as I am, put the box on your lap and do it much as a ventriloquist act. The children will not care if they see you talk for the puppet. Your voice should be clear, pleasantly pitched, and easy to understand; it does not need to be disguised. Avoid sounding false, high pitched, or whiny.

Ko-Ko's "good-bye" can be followed with a fingerplay, such as:

> The Holy Bible is God's Book,
>   (*hands together, closed*)
> Let's open it and see,
>   (*open hands, palms up*)
> The story we will hear today,
> A story for you and me.
>   (*point to someone and then to self*)

Follow this with, "When we open the Bible today we find the story of . . . ," and then present the Bible story.

Be prepared! Practice at least once aloud and in front of a mirror. Be sure of yourself so that you are not tied to your book. Be enthusiastic and use vivacious facial expressions. Don't forget to use your hands. Vary the story presentation. Display a large picture and point out the characters as you tell the story, or you may utilize the flannelgraph board and put on the pictures as you progress with the story. At other times use the "Show and Tell" projector to present the lesson. Rather than listening to the recording, three-year-olds may enjoy the Show and Tell stories more if you narrate the story yourself. Or you may borrow one of the well-illustrated Arch Book Series (Concordia Publishing) from the library and read from it. This series has a new, fresh presentation of Bible stories. Read the story from the book, but hold it to the side of you so the children can see the pictures at all times. Know the story so you can read it from the side without moving the book in front of you. With a little practice this can be done easily. On another morning you can draw a very light sketch of a picture on a piece of paper and fill in with a magic marker as you tell the Bible story. If you are especially talented in this area, draw the picture free hand as you talk, but if not, use light lines as your guide. For another variation present the story as a puppet show. Use flannelboard characters and mount them on sticks to do a simple puppet presentation. These are stick puppets which can be held up to "walk," just appearing over the edge of a table. After this is done once, children will like to take a puppet and manipulate it as you retell the story.

The storytime is important. Your attitude must express this to the children. Make them realize that these are real stories. You can ask, "Is this a real or a pretend story?" and "How do you know?" ("Because it is from the Bible.") Also ask these questions with a story used later in the morning. In response to "How do you know?" they may reply, "Because the animals talked. . . ." They can soon sift out the real from the pretend with your help.

As you give the story presentation, maintain continuity by avoiding interruptions. If a child interrupts, ask him to wait until the story is over or tell him, "Not now." When too many children talk or the teacher attempts to answer all their questions, the interest of most of the children is lost.

The storytime can be closed with a simple prayer.

Special activity time. Before the children move to the table, the teacher can demonstrate the special activity for the day. This special activity is an excellent opportunity for expressing the Bible truths through some type of art or craft activity. It is crucial that the child does as much of this project as possible. The *doing* is the important thing, so do not feel that the finished product has to be a thing of beauty. If the prepared projects that accompany your lessons are too complicated, switch to providing your own with coloring, chalk, pasting, or collages; but keep them simple.

Children can share large crayons from discarded margarine dishes. One child can share paste from a container with three others, but each child should have his own dull-pointed scissors for cutting.

On some days the special activity can be acting out the Bible story as you retell it. This may be done with a few children at a time or with all participating, moving about the room easily and casually.

If this period includes a light snack, use this opportunity to teach the children a prayer of grace. One of my favorites is:

> Thank you, God, for things to eat,
> For things to do and see.
> But most of all for people,
> Who take good care of me.

Singing Time. Let the children gather on the rug and sing songs. Use simple songs and pitch them in a medium range. A piano is not necessary. Preschoolers sing very well without accompaniment. Teach the children songs that everyone knows, like the old favorites they will hear and sing all through their lives. Then teach them new songs that you find delightful. Use song charts to help the children picture the words of the song. This adds meaning and helps them learn the song quickly. A song chart is a big piece of paper with pictures for the key words of the song.

For example:

> Jesus listens when I pray,
> When I pray, when I pray.

Jesus listens when I pray,
Every night, every day.

Use a picture of Jesus, then a picture of a child praying, and then a moon and sun, and point to the appropriate pictures for "Jesus," "When I pray," and "Every night, every day." Song charts can also be made as a book, a wheel that turns, or in any other form. After a few times let one of the children point as other children sing the song.

Fingerplays are a learning and doing activity. They are very meaningful to a child as he does the actions and says Bible truths. Select one new fingerplay for one Sunday and then repeat it for several weeks. Let the children listen and imitate your movements as soon as they wish. After the first time, tell them to say as much as they can remember with you. Repeat fingerplays, for children love repetition. This is something they can remember and carry home and tell their parents and sisters and brothers. They are easy to remember because of the rhymes and the rhythm. It will be necessary for you to know them thoroughly and tell them. Books of fingerplays specifically written for Sunday schools are available at religious book stores. Your own Sunday school materials may include some that you can use.

During these last minutes, when you have time, you can use David C. Cook's "Winky the Bear" flannelgraph stories. Winky is a paper puppet bear that comes with flannelgraph pictures. You hold Winky in one hand and add the appropriate figures to the board as you tell the story. Children love him and his daily activities. Winky is much like them and has many things to learn about good living. The stories are brief and can be easily told in your own words, after you get the story idea. David C. Cook has many Winky stories, along with sets about "Frisky and the Turnabout Twins."

This last period of time is designed to be flexible. You choose the activities that you have time for, to dismiss at the proper time. You will not be left with empty minutes or be struggling to finish a project while the parents are arriving. A cheery "Good-bye, we were so glad you came," and "See you next week" and the morning has passed quickly and profitably.

In carrying out a preschool program many people have questions about how to discipline small children in a group. Mix firmness with kindness. Love them, know them, and treat them individually.

Check your physical surroundings. Are the chairs too large? Is the table at a comfortable height? There should be a rug for the children to be seated on for storytime. Children are much more comfortable seated on the floor for these activities. If you have a carpeted room, you are all set. Otherwise, buy a washable oval or round rug that is large enough for your children to sit along the edge in a circle, with you on a low chair at one end. Carpet squares are also excellent to use. They can be conveniently stacked in the room, and each child can take a square and put it on the floor. The children's comfort minimizes discipline.

Sometimes you must say no to a child, but say it simply and matter-of-factly. You might say, "That's a rule," or "That's what we do here." Do not make long explanations.

If a child does not want to participate, you cannot force him. Let him watch until he is comfortable. You may be able to ease him into participation with your support by standing near him, letting him sit with you, or quietly reassuring him.

Keep every minute of the session filled. Have those extras ready for extra time. For restlessness during any time of the morning, be ready with stretching exercises such as wiggling fingers; moving arms; touching head, shoulders, knees, and toes. These exercises can be found in books for preschoolers. Some can be sung or just chanted. When children begin touching someone else and picking at them, it is time for some stretching.

If children are distracted during the lesson, try to touch them gently if you can reach them, without stopping your telling of the story. If you have a helper, she can sit with the children and do this to bring them back quietly. If the child cannot be reached, simply insert his name in the story—for example: "As the beggar walked down the road, *Johnny,* he saw a man who was. . . ." The sound of his name will recapture his attention and he will look at you and listen again.

Be ready with your projects. Hunting for your supplies while the children are waiting at the table causes discipline problems.

Always have a plan. Children like and need a routine. On days when the usual program cannot be followed, say, "Today is a special day and we are not going to have Ko-Ko time, but we will have a story and then we will go with other boys and girls to sing."

Know your material. You cannot fool even young children. You must be very interested or they will not be. Be enthusiastic and they will be!

Preschoolers are not miniature adults, so let there be no miniature Sunday schools. Make your preschool hour a time of real, meaningful spiritual experiences for the young child.

> Eagerly the child comes in,
> Not knowing what he'll see.
> He looks trustingly at you and says,
> "Here I am, teach me!"

9 BUILDING AND USING THE CHURCH LIBRARY FOR SUNDAY SCHOOL

Joanne Boehm

One of the major purposes of the Sunday school is to instruct its pupils in the Word of God. This is a challenging task; however, like most worthwhile endeavors, it is not an easy one, especially today. Our students are exposed to many new ideas and learning media. They receive new ideas through other media such as television, radio, tapes, records, or other forms of audio-visual instruction. Their minds are challenged by these forms of education. Many third graders handle their encyclopedias and cassette players as confidently as the older generation the newspaper.

Obviously, Sunday school teachers face a tremendous challenge; and often they have had little or no training for the task the church has asked them to perform. The teachers, consequently, need help and much preparation if they are to do their task effectively. This is not, however, an impossible

---

Joanne Boehm, Grand Rapids, Michigan, is the librarian at the Reformed Bible College, member of the Cascade Christian Reformed library committee, and workshop instructor in church librarianship.

task. The benefits of the book explosion as well as all the new media are not only available to the pupils, but also to the Sunday school staff. Just as for the pupils, so for the leaders, there is an unlimited amount of material available to those who want to prepare themselves adequately. In doing so, they are helping themselves to improve their teaching and in that way better serve those whom they teach. The difficulty for most teachers is how to know what are the best materials, where they are to be obtained, and how they can be financed. Here is where the church library can be of tremendous value.

One of the main functions of the church library is to support and strengthen the Christian education program. This means that the church librarian should obtain the best materials available for this purpose, prepare and record them in such a way that they are readily available, and circulate them among all the groups and individuals in the church concerned with the education program, including the Sunday school.

The church library can help the Sunday school staff in many different ways. For example, the new superintendent may want to know what are his duties, how the Sunday school should be organized, how teachers should be selected and trained, and how special programs should be organized. Books are available that can give guidance for this work and should become a part of the church library. Furthermore, filmstrips, records, and pamphlets are available to help the superintendent in instructing his teachers how to teach in the Sunday school and how to understand the pupils better. A choice selection of Christmas programs in the church library may save the superintendent and the staff much time and effort in deciding which program to use. These are just some suggestions in which the church library and librarian can serve.

For the teacher, books which give information concerning specific characteristics and interests of a certain age group will be important. The approach to a kindergarten class should be different than the approach to a group of second graders. Lesson planning for a young people's group should vary from that for an adult group. There are books that teach how to tell stories, how to lead discussion groups, how to teach with pictures, maps, slides, filmstrips, flannelgraph, records, tapes, and how to use audio-visual equipment such as projectors, tape recorders, and overhead projectors.

For lesson preparation, several good translations of the Bible, Bible story books, an atlas, dictionary, concordance, commentary, and a Bible history book should be available to help the teacher. For teaching the lesson, the teacher may have decided to use pictures, recordings, or other forms of teaching aids. All these types of books and materials should be found in the church library.

Another way the library can be of help to the teacher and the pupils is to give the pupils research projects to do for which they can use the church library. If that type of assignment is given, it is well to plan such a project together with the church librarian so that sufficient material will be at hand and she is prepared to be of help to the students. The librarian may be asked to show and explain the use of the library and certain materials to the class so that the students will get to know their library.

Most Sunday schools have a director in charge of the song service. It would be good, therefore, to have one or two good children's hymn books in the library. To help the song leader in teaching new songs, some records or visualized songs would be helpful so that tunes and words may be learned quickly. The song leader should at times give the background information on how these great hymns and carols came to be written. A reliable book on hymnology will be valuable for this purpose.

It is quite evident that the church library can be of vital importance to the Sunday school program, and therefore more and more churches are realizing the need of a close working relationship between the Sunday school staff and the librarian. Too often, however, in many Sunday schools the staff is not aware of the many services the library offers. Many teachers do not realize what can be found in their library.

Even though many church librarians would like to fill their shelves with material that will help the Sunday school, they find to their discouragement that the teachers never ask for a book that will help them in their lesson preparation. Since usually church library budgets are small, and librarians get many requests for new children's books, Christian novels, and biography, it is understandable that a large percentage of the money will be used to obtain materials for which there is demand. Do not be surprised, therefore, if your church library at present does not have all the different types of materials listed in this chapter. The library, however, probably has more books to aid the Sunday school teacher than he is aware of.

To build up the church library to such an extent that it can adequately fulfill its function of strengthening and supporting the educational program of the church is a task which should be worked at in earnest, for it gives blessed rewards. This goal will not be realized overnight, nor will it ever be completely attained because it is a continuous process. With the effort of some interested and concerned members of the church, however, much can be accomplished to improve the church library in a short time. Many churches can witness to that fact and it might be worthwhile if a visit was paid to other libraries. Librarians in your community will gladly assist you if you call on them.

In order to develop an adequate church library, there needs to be a conviction of the worthwhileness of such an endeavor. To accomplish the goals of a good church library, there is need for a librarian who is dedicated, has the ability to secure reliable helpers, and can handle the task enthusiastically. Even though a person may be inexperienced at first, study and workshop courses will help her to become a proficient librarian.

Next, the church needs to budget funds so that the program of the library can be developed and maintained to serve all its functions.

The librarian should be informed about all the activities of the Sunday school well in advance of the time they are to be carried out, so that helpful material may be made available to support these activities. At times it will be necessary to locate, order, and prepare materials for circulation. This means that the librarian should be kept informed which lessons the different Sunday school classes will be covering the following season. It would be well to discuss with the librarian what materials will be needed at what date and what is available now in the library or what should be obtained for this purpose before the date of use. Reservations for audio-visual equipment such as filmstrip and overhead projectors, record players, and other equipment should also be made well in advance.

Another way in which the library can be improved is by giving to the librarian suggestions of new materials which may be helpful to others. The librarian has the task of serving the total church program, and since she cannot be an expert in all the areas of this program, suggestions or information where to obtain good materials needed in the library will help to build your church library. Therefore, good cooperation between the Sunday school staff and the church librarian can be of tremendous value in your teaching program.

Because the librarian in a church program is so strategic, it may be advisable to have her at the curriculum planning or periodic business meeting of the Sunday school, and even now and then at the consistory meeting of the church for suggestions, progress reports, and overall consultation.

To start a collection of books which will be valuable to the Sunday school staff and as a beginning guide, the following books are suggested for building the church library for the Sunday school staff:

Books for lesson preparations

Bibles

It is taken for granted that you have several different translations of the Bible for comparison and study purposes.

Commentaries:

Erdman, Charles R., *Exposition of the Bible.* Philadelphia: Westminster Press

Henry, Matthew, *Commentary on the Whole Bible.* Grand Rapids: Zondervan

General Works

Blaiklock, E. M., *Zondervan's Pictorial Atlas.* Grand Rapids: Zondervan

Edersheim, Alfred, *The Bible History (Old Testament).* Grand Rapids: Eerdmans

Edersheim, Alfred, *The Life and Times of Jesus the Messiah.* Grand Rapids: Eerdmans

Douglas, J. D., ed., *The New Bible Dictionary.* Grand Rapids: Eerdmans

Northcott, William Cecil, *Bible Encyclopedia for Children.* Philadelphia: Westminster Press

Young, Robert, *Analytical Concordance to the Bible.* Grand Rapids: Eerdmans

Northcott, William Cecil, *Bible Encyclopedia for Children.* Philadelphia: Westminster Press

Young, Robert, *Analytical Concordance to the Bible.* Grand Rapids: Eerdmans

Children's Story Bibles

Egermeier, Elsie Emilie, *Bible Story Book.* Anderson, Ind.: Warner Press

Haan, Sheri, *Good News for Children.* Grand Rapids: Baker Book House

Korfker, Dena, *My Picture Story Bible.* Grand Rapids: Zondervan

Schoolland, Marian M., *Marian's Book of Bible Stories.* Grand Rapids: Eerdmans

Vos, Catherine Frances, *The Child's Story Bible.* Grand Rapids: Eerdmans

Practical Helps for the Sunday School Staff

Benson, Clarence H., *Christian Teacher.* Chicago: Moody Press

Benson, Clarence H., *An Introduction to Child Study.* Chicago: Moody Press

Eavey, Charles B., *Principles of Teaching for Christian Teachers*. Grand Rapids: Zondervan

Jones, Idris W., *Superintendent Plans His Work*. Valley Forge, Penn.: Judson Press

Keekley, Weldon, *Church School Superintendent*. St. Louis: Bethany Press

Leavitt, Gary P., *Teach with Success*. Cincinnati: Standard Publishing

Salisbury, Hugh M. and Peabody, Larry, *Guide to Effective Bible Teaching*. Grand Rapids: Baker

Woodworth, R. O., *How to Operate a Sunday School*. Grand Rapids: Zondervan

Music

Bailey, Albert E., *The Gospel in Hymns*. New York: Charles Scribner's Sons

Daves, Michael, *Famous Hymns and Their Writers*. Old Tappan, N.J.: Fleming H. Revell

Hamersma, John, ed., *Hymns for Youth*. Grand Rapids: National Union of Christian Schools

Vander Baan, Wilma, ed., *The Children's Hymnbook*. Grand Rapids: National Union of Christian Schools

Book Publishers

Baker Book House
1019 Wealthy St., S.E.
Grand Rapids, Mich. 49506

Bethany Press
Box 179
St. Louis, Mo. 63166

Moody Press
820 N. La Salle St.
Chicago, Ill. 60610

Wm. B. Eerdmans Publishing Company
255 Jefferson Ave. S.E.
Grand Rapids, Mich. 49502

Judson Press
Valley Forge, Pa. 19481

Standard Publishing
8121 Hamilton AVe.
Cincinnati, Ohio 45231

National Union of
Christian Schools
865 - 28th St. S.E.
Grand Rapids, Mich. 49508

Fleming H. Revell Company
Old Tappan, N.J. 07675

Charles Scribner's Sons
597 Fifth Ave.
New York, N.Y. 10017

Warner Press
1200 E. 5th St.
Anderson, Ind. 46011

Westminster Press
Witherspoon Bldg.
Juniper and Walnut Sts.
Philadelphia, Pa. 19107

Zondervan Publishing House
1415 Lake Drive S.E.
Grand Rapids, Mich. 49506

Audio-Visual Materials

For teacher training, the following audio-visual kits will be valuable: Building a Better Sunday School, Successful Teaching, Know Your Child.

These kits contain filmstrips, records, and manual. Write for catalog and prices to: Moody Institute of Science, Educational Film Division, 12000 E. Washington Blvd., Whittier, Calif. 90606.

There is also a set of nine records available titled *Basic Teacher Training*. They can be obtained from Gospel Light Publications, Glendale, California.

To teach the Bible stories using visual aids, the following publishers are recommended. Write for a catalog to the following addresses: Church Craft, Visual Data Corp., Chesterfield, Mo. 63017. This company has an extensive collection of slides, filmstrips, and stori-strips based on stories of the Bible. Stori-strips are inexpensive. They are good for small group showings but not for larger groups. The stori-strip projector is inexpensive and can be purchased from this company also. However, if you already have a filmstrip projector, an adapter can also be obtained for a few dollars.

Other sources for filmstrips are: Concordia Publishing House, 3558 S. Jefferson Ave., St. Louis, Mo. 63118. Cathedral filmstrips can be obtained through your local audio-visual dealer, where you also may inquire about Church Craft materials, Concordia filmstrips, and Moody filmstrips.

Newman Visual Education, Inc., 400 - 32nd St. S.E., Grand Rapids, Mich. will also be able to obtain some of these materials for you.

Moody filmstrips of Bible stories can also be obtained at Moody Institute of Science (see the address above).

For flannelgraph stories, Scripture Press's collection on Bible stories is highly recommended: Scripture Press, 1825 College Ave., Wheaton, Ill. 60187.

For more flannelgraph materials, pictures, maps, and visualized songs, visit your local store that deals in Sunday school materials, or ask for a catalog of Sunday school supplies from:

Kregel's Bookstore		Zondervan Publishing House
P.O. Box 2607	or	1415 Lake Dr. S.E.
Grand Rapids, Mich. 49501		Grand Rapids, Mich. 49506

10 SEEING IS BELIEVING—LOOK AND LEARN FROM VISUAL AIDS

Elaine Mannes and Jennie De Roos

"We haven't had Bible club for two weeks. Who can retell the Bible story we discussed the last time we met?" inquired the teacher. After some thought a junior boy volunteered the answer, accurately recounting many details of the story of Noah and the ark. How could this boy—an unchurched lad who had only that one time heard this Scripture story—remember so many of the details? The reason: a visual aid had been used during the lesson presentation the previous week.

What is a visual aid?

A visual aid is an object, symbol, or picture that appeals to the sense of sight. To be effective, visual aids should be simple, correlated, and well prepared. Their purpose is to secure the pupils' attention and hold their interest. Visual

---

Elaine Mannes and Jennie De Roos, Denver, Colorado, have been leaders and lecturers in Sunday school in Denver for many years.

aids are in two categories: projected (such as filmstrips and movies) and nonprojected (charts, objects, or models).

Why use visual aids?

Educators have proved that learning potential is increased when students see as well as hear the subject material. We who are involved in religious education ought to exploit this fact, using the eye as well as the ear to implant Scripture in our students' minds, using aids to set the stage for learning, to clarify a thought, or to make the abstract clear.

Consider the following when choosing a visual aid:

1. *The age of the pupils.* Certain types of visual aids are more appropriate for one age group than for another. For this reason become familiar with the physical and mental characteristics of the pupils you are teaching. Know, for example, that map study has much appeal for a fourth grader but is useless for a preschooler.

2. *The number of students in the class.* Select a visual aid that can be seen by every member in the group. Interest is quickly lost when some of the students are unable to see every part of the aid. For this reason some of the materials in purchased visual aid packets may have to be enlarged for use in your particular room.

3. *The space available.* Many classrooms are not large enough for using projected visual aids, or perhaps the sound effects of such an audio-visual may be disturbing to a nearby class. Consider combining many classes for the showing of such an aid and then form small buzz groups for discussion time.

4. *Time for preparation and practice.* Essential to good Sunday school teaching is the time teachers spend delving into the Word of God, gleaning its truths. Always allow yourself time first of all for adequate preparation and then for planning and preparing the teaching aid.

5. *Availability of materials.* Become completely oriented to the materials your Sunday school has available. Or if you

are preparing an original visual demonstration, you may need to file the idea for later use if materials, such as flannelgraph or flat pictures, are not available for making this particular aid workable for the current lesson.

6. *Equipment available.* Know what equipment your school has, such as flannelboards, easels (both floor and table), projection equipment (slides, filmstrips, movies, overhead machine, and transparencies, Phono-viewer, and opaque projector), and display boards and tables. If your organization requires making reservation for use of equipment and materials, make sure you do this well ahead of the date you need it.

7. *When was a similar aid used last?* Variety in using teaching aids is important if a high level of student interest is to be maintained.

When can visual aids be used?

Use visual aids throughout the Sunday school hour, motivating students to become actively involved in the total program. Consider using visual aids as your assistant for making an attractive room atmosphere, during departmental worship time, for the Bible lesson, and in Scripture memorization.

Creating room atmosphere

Create an exciting atmosphere by using bulletin boards and interest-center displays in department rooms, classrooms, and hallways. For durability purchase boards for this purpose. If finances are limited, make bulletin boards from large pieces of corrugated cardboard that appliances are shipped in. If you are using this latter suggestion, stain the pieces of cardboard with wood stain; then frame the boards with two- to three-inch-wide strips of plastic adhesive, such as Contact. Mount bulletin boards to the wall or display on easels.

Purchase ready-made interest centers or make your own. A very inexpensive classroom interest table can be made by bolting a piece of plywood to the top of a discarded four-legged television stand. Remove the casters from the stand, add a plywood top that is larger than the actual dimensions of the stand; then cover the plywood with paint, a wood stain, or plastic adhesive material.

Display boards should always be purposeful and attractive. Use bulletin boards to teach Biblical truths, emphasize special days or seasons, stress home or foreign missions, and to give continuity to an individual lesson or unit of study.

Use an assortment of media for bulletin board backgrounds, such as construction or crepe paper, cloth (cotton, taffeta, felt, or burlap), or colorful corrugated paper (available in stationery stores and school supply houses). Occasionally edge the board with scalloped or pointed strips of corrugated paper. Cut letters for captions from construction paper or cover lightweight cardboard letters with pieces of colored foil gift wrap. Unusual letters are made by dipping pieces of heavy string in undiluted starch and then forming the moistened string into the desired shape. Let the forms dry on aluminum foil before using. Also make letters using a series of thumb tacks or upholstery nails or by pinning individually wrapped pieces of candy to the board. Vary the size and shape of letters. Use letter stencils or draw freehand.

Carry out the theme of the board by using flat pictures, in true-to-life colors. (A picture file is a "must" for all teachers. Collect pictures from magazines like *Ideals, Arizona Highways,* and religious periodicals. Also purchase picture packets from religious publishers.) Actual objects can also be attached to the board. For example a cluster of Indian corn or clusters of grapes pinned to a fall board arrangement adds beauty. Use paper silhouettes or children's drawings. Boards assembled using only black and white materials are very unusual and striking.

Bulletin board ideas can be copied or original. Visit day schools and adapt secular board ideas to fit your needs in the church school. Read books of bulletin board suggestions. (See bibliography at end of chapter 11.) Ideas for original boards are often inspired from magazine covers, greeting cards, or they may be formed as you read Scripture or sing a song.

Assemble an interest-center arrangement that correlates with the bulletin board theme. Display objects like candles, sea shells, rocks, flowers (fresh or artificial), pictures, or other theme related materials. For example, when teaching the lesson of Mary and Martha, based on Luke 10:38-42, display a table setting on one side of the interest table and an opened Bible on the opposite side. Complete the display with a provocative placard with the words WHO SERVED BEST? printed on it. Or during the Lenten season flank a styrofoam or wooden cross with white lilies. Make a crown of thorns by soaking Russian olive branches in water until bendable and then forming them into a circle. Tie the crown together with wire, around the crossbar of the cross.

Add color to the interest table by setting the objects on a piece of colored cloth (chiffon, velvet, cotton, or nylon net). Drape the material similar to the style used in department store displays.

Visual aids during the worship time

Regardless of the students' age, visual aids add intrigue and meaning to the opening worship period. Again consider using aids already prepared by Sunday school supply houses, or make one of your own design.

For pupils who can read, sometimes begin the worship period with a Call to Worship chart, read in unison, alerting the students to the presence of God. Draw a large opened Bible (19" x 15") on white posterboard. (If the posterboard is white on both sides it has double use.) Paint the edges of the Bible shape black and red, representing the cover and edges of a Bible. Cut out the Bible shape. Print the words of an appropriate Bible verse on the poster. (When you have collected several visualized verses, assemble them into a flip chart, using ring binders at the top to hold the pages together.)

Use visualized song charts during worship time. If your Sunday school department has a large repertory of visuals—either handmade or purchased—weekly selections will be greater since you need not be limited to selecting songs found in books your Sunday school has in quantity or depend on songs your pupils have memorized. Consider printing (a combination of both capital and lower case letters) the words of songs on large sheets or posterboard, on song related shapes, flashcards, blank spiral books, or transparencies for overhead projection. Song related pictures will enhance the appearance of song visuals. Some songs can be pictured on flannelboard. The song "When He Cometh" (*Youth Worship and Sing*, p. 236) is such an example. Draw a large crown. Cut the crown from gold felt. Make five jewels—four of one size and one larger for the center of the crown. Cut out five photographs of children; glue to the center of the jewels. Outline each jewel and areas of the crown with white glue and sprinkle generously with glitter. After the glue has dried shake off excess glitter. When using the visual, display the completed crown on the flannelboard. A dark green felt background will offset a gold crown. Place the jewels on the crown.

Slides, both purchased and ones from a private collection, can sometimes be used to correlate with a hymn, making the message more meaningful to the pupils. The following slides are available from Society for Visual Education, Inc., 1345 Diversey Parkway, Chicago, Illinois 60614, and are suggested for use with the hymn "One Day" (*Let Youth Praise Him*, p. 67). Send to SVE for a current price sheet.

> Ha 722—Angels Announce the Glad Tidings—Verse 1
> Ha 46—Jesus Dies for Us—Verse 2
> N 214—The Burial of Jesus—Verse 3
> Ha 47—The Resurrection—Verse 4
> Hc 32—Open Bible

Project slides of your own choosing for viewing during the refrain. If your students are not familiar with the words of the song, obtain a soloist to sing each of the verses with audience participation on the chorus. At the conclusion of the song project a handmade slide with the thought-provoking question ARE YOU READY? printed on it. (For making this slide, purchase a blank slide and print the words on it with a ball-point pen.) Allow time for the students to think about this question slide while the pianist plays softly in the background; then lead your pupils in a moment of prayer.

Sometimes introduce songs that recall a Bible story by dramatically telling that particular Biblical account, enhanced by using flannelgraph or felt-o-graph. To illustrate, tell the Bible stories of *Blind Bartimaeus*, *The Demoniac Healed*, and *The Garden of Gethsemane*, interspersed with singing "Then Jesus Came" (*Let Youth Praise Him*, p. 69). Many songs, especially those emphasizing special Christian holidays, can be used with the story-telling method. Cassette tapes can be used for background music also.

Use visualized stories that stress missions or those that help to build Christian character during the worship hour. Purchase stories and visuals from religious book stores, or write directly to such organizations as the American Bible Society, P.O. Box 5656, Grand Central Station, New York, N.Y. 10017, or from World Vision, Inc., P.O. Box O, Pasadena, Calif., to find out what materials they have available for Sunday school teachers.

In addition to using pictures in telling a story, sometimes the storyteller herself can become the visual aid by dressing in a costume similar to that worn by the main character in the story.

SEEING IS BELIEVING—HELPS AND HINTS FOR USING VISUAL AIDS

Elaine Mannes and Jennie De Roos

In the previous chapter, some questions such as "What is a visual aid?" and "Why use visual aids?" were considered and answered. In this chapter, further helps and hints will be presented to make your use of visual aids more effective and meaningful.

Use, but do not limit your choice of aids to include only those suggested in your teacher's manual or those which come in a publisher's visual aid packet. Let your own creativity be exercised, fashioning your own aids which especially fulfill the needs of your students. Rarely discard a visual idea because it doesn't seem workable for the current subject material. Rather, rework the idea for the current lesson or file the thought for later use when the idea more adequately fits the subject matter.

Use meaningful visual aids for the lesson approach or introduction, capturing the attention of each student, setting the stage for learning. The following visualized lesson introductions are for you to use, as well as samples to serve as guidelines for thinking visually concerning lesson introductions. The first sample is an introduction for *Jesus or Barabbas,* Matthew 27:11-20.

1. The materials you need are: A balloon. (Have an extra one too, in case one pops.) A dime wrapped between two circles of cardboard. (Aluminum foil works well for wrapping paper.) A straight pin. A Bible. (When you finish with the point of contact, take your Bible in hand as you tell the events of this lesson.)

"Nearly all of us, I'm sure, have seen television programs where many awards were given to the contestants. Sometimes a contestant needs to make a *choice,* deciding if he wants to keep the gift he has already won or take a chance and give it up for something unknown. Often the contestant makes a good *choice* and gets something much more valuable than he had already won—like trading a box of buttons for a brand-new car. Sometimes, though, the contestant makes a bad *choice* and has to give up a valuable possession.

"Before I came to Sunday school this morning I made a *choice.* I decided to take something unusual to class. [Hold up the balloon into which the wrapped dime has been inserted and inflate it.] Look! there's something in my balloon. I wonder what it is. Who would like to have this balloon? I see by looking at your hands you've all made a *choice.* Some of you have decided you want the balloon and have raised your hands to show this. Some of you kept your hands down, which makes me think you wouldn't care for this balloon. [Give the balloon away. Ask the receiver if he wants to break the balloon and get the special gift that is in it immediately. Let public opinion sway the child's decision. If the child decides to keep the balloon, do all you can to persuade him to break it so he can open the gift immediately. If the child breaks the balloon, continue with this paragraph, otherwise skip down to the next paragraph.]

"Oh, look now, [name the child] has another *choice* to make. I wonder if [name the child] will decide to open the gift and let us all see what it is? Boys and girls, do you want to see what it is? [Again let the group sway the child's decision. If the child opens the gift, tell the group he still has another important *choice* to make. He must decide if he will spend all the money for himself or give part of it to the church for a tithe. Then continue:]

"Life is full of *choices*—some are important, while others really don't make any difference in the way we decide. In our lesson the people had to make an important *choice* too. They were told by the leaders of the people to decide if they wanted to free Barabbas, a murderer, or let Jesus, the innocent one, go free.

"Let's all sit very quietly now for the Bible lesson—in fact, so still that we can hear this pin drop." (Hold up a pin and drop it to the floor in order to gain the children's undivided attention. Continue to tell the Bible story with much enthusiasm, using group response during the presentation.)

2. Capture the junior and junior high students' attention by using a mock newspaper headline as the lesson approach.

On a piece of newsprint paper print the words of a catchy lesson title. For example, for the lesson on *Jesus' Second Coming* from I Thessalonians 3:1-6; 4:13-18, use the title JESUS IS COMING! ARE YOU READY?; or for *Jairus's Daughter Healed*, Matthew 9:18-26, use the title DOCTOR'S HOUSE CALL INTERRUPTED. PATIENT DIES! After printing the title, paste the strip of paper over the headlines of your local newspaper. Display the newspaper after they are assembled.

3. This startling introduction can be used as the approach to any Bible lesson. Hold up your Bible and say: "This book isn't worth the paper it's printed on. At least that's what I heard someone say the other day. But I know that statement isn't true. This is the blessed Word of God, the Word handed down from generation to generation—first from father to son and later the words were recorded in a book.

"Yes, this book is true—every word. It is the infallible Word of God. Today we will be studying from [give Scripture reference and continue with the lesson using a method of your choice.]"

Many visual aids can be used during the Bible lesson presentation. Some of these aids include the flannelgraph, plastic flip charts (see bibliography at end of this chapter), objects, models, chalkboard illustrations, flashcards, filmstrips, movies, and overhead projection.

In addition to purchasing flannelgraph packets that directly correlate with the Bible lessons, sometimes use picture sequence flannelgraph lessons. For this kind of a visual presentation find flannel backed pictures or make symbol and word cards (backed with flannel) that depict the story events. To illustrate: For the lesson based on Luke 15, *The Lost Sheep,* use these figures: a shepherd, 100, sheep, P.M., 99, and a lost sheep on the shoulders of the shepherd. Place the figures on the board as you tell the parable. Also let the children use the figures as they retell the story.

Lesson related objects can be elaborate or simple. Take a bag of rags to class when teaching the lesson from Jeremiah 38, *Jeremiah Saved from the Dungeon.* As you display the rags at the right moment, most children will be impressed with the kindness shown by the black man as the Old Testament prophet was lifted from the pit.

Bible stories take on added meaning for young children when objects are used with the story-telling method. Wear a Bible-times headdress (made from a large square of cloth and pinned on the head) when telling the story of *Hannah's Prayer,* I Samuel 1. As you come to the climax of the story, take from hiding a doll, representing baby Samuel, wrapped in a blanket and show the "baby" to the children. Allow the children to handle the objects following the story presentation.

Objects can be used as a lesson application. The following is such an example and correlates with Bible passages stressing sin. Before class time place the following things in a red, heart shaped box: a stone, a stick, a small broken toy, some money, a candy wrapper, a picture of an unhappy child, a piece of modeling clay, a picture of Jesus, of a child singing, of a child listening to a Bible story, of a child sharing, and of a child praying. Place the objects and pictures in reverse order in the heart box.

Hold the box in your hands and ask the children to identify what it is you are holding and are about to open. Then proceed by telling them that not every heart is filled with love, because some people do not know Jesus.

> "This heart is that of Tom, a boy who lives in the neighborhood. He is a rough boy and he has no friends. Even his parents do not love him. Let's open this heart that is filled with hate and sin and see how it makes Tom act toward others. [Open heart, hold up stone.] A stone! And

that is how Tom's heart was; it was filled with sin. He would throw stones at other boys and girls to hurt them. Sometimes he even broke windows by throwing stones.

"Here is a stick. [Hold up stick.] Tom used a stick to hit the pets of his neighbors and he chased smaller children with it.

"Let's look some more in this sinful heart. [Hold up the toy.] A broken toy! Tom liked to sneak into other children's play yards to break their toys or take them away from the children.

(Hold up money.) "This money was taken from his mother's purse without asking. That is stealing, but Tom didn't know it was wrong to steal. [Show the candy wrapper.] Candy is so tasty, and Tom would swipe some from the grocery store. That is also stealing. [Hold up picture of unhappy child.] This boy looks so unhappy, and that is how Tom looked.

"One day Johnnie asked Tom to come with him to Sunday school. At first Tom said no, but the closer it came to Sunday he began to think about the invitation. He didn't have any Sunday clothes, and he wondered if the other children would like him. Johnnie had prayed for Tom every night because he wanted Tom to be kind and happy. Tom got up early Sunday and dressed in clean clothes. Off to Johnnie's house he ran, hoping he would go to Sunday school. Johnnie was happy to see him and took him by the hand.

"At Sunday school, Tom heard for the first time, 'Jesus Loves Me.' Could it be that someone really loved him? [Show picture of Jesus.] No one had told him this before. He could hardly wait to go to Sunday school with Johnnie again. His heart was becoming soft like clay. [Hold up clay.]

"The next Sunday Tom joined the children in singing. He learned how to be kind, helpful, and to share. [Hold up picture of child sharing.]

"The teacher sent a little prayer home with him, which he learned. Tom was a changed boy and he asked God to forgive the bad things he had done. Satan no longer ruled Tom's life."

Mold a clay model of Dagon, god of the Philistines, when teaching from Judges 16:23. Form softened clay into the head, arms, and shoulders of a man, with the body tapering away into the form of a fish. Use the completed model to demonstrate the foolishness of idol worship. Remove Dagon's head (I Sam. 5:3, 4) to show how God became provoked with the Philistines concerning the ark.

The chalkboard can be used with every age group because of its unlimited possibilities for visualizing Biblical truths. Use simple stick figures or detailed drawings depicting an entire scene. Use words, captions, or print the lesson outline on the board for the students to follow. If your classroom is not equipped with a chalkboard, use a piece of newsprint paper. (Tablets or individual sheets of newsprint paper are available in artist or stationery stores.) Place newsprint tablet on an easel, or tape a sheet of newsprint to the wall. For a pleasing effect use pastel-colored chalk. If you do not have the knack to draw freehand, predraw your material, using light lines, before class time.

Bible lesson flashcards are useful. Draw pictures, symbols, and words on pieces of posterboard. The following flashcard suggestion visualizes a life related application for *The Confession of Thomas,* John 20:19-29. Prepare five flashcards as follows: a hand with a pointing finger, a heart with the word DOUBT, a heart with the word SIN, a heart labeled with specific sins as suggested in the script, and a cross.

> Flashcard 1: "Boys and girls, we often point our finger at Thomas and exclaim that he was a very doubting person."
>
> Flashcard 2: "We say, 'Oh, Thomas, your heart was filled with DOUBT.' Remember, when we point our finger accusingly at Thomas we have three fingers pointing back at us."
>
> Flashcard 3: "We need to ask ourselves a very important question. What SIN is in my heart?"
>
> Flashcard 4: "Do we have trouble with *nasty* thoughts or saying *bad words* when we get angry? Are we more *interested in getting things for ourselves* than giving unselfishly to others? Do we ever yield to temptation? Like when we go into a grocery store and no one is looking at us when we go past the candy counter? Is *cheating* our problem? Do we always say no to temptation when we don't know the answer on a test and we could so easily look over someone's shoulder and use his answer? Do we lie? Are we *mean* to a

schoolmate who acts differently from the other kids? If we are honest with ourselves we will see some of these sins in our own lives. There is Someone who will help us. . . . "

Flashcard 5: "His name is Jesus. Jesus died on the *cross* to save us from our sins. When we believe in Jesus Christ He will cleanse our hearts, helping us to stand firm against temptation. Let us bow in prayer now and ask Jesus to help us."

Help your students memorize and understand Scripture through visual aids. Learning potential is measurably increased when the eye and ear gate are used to teach a Bible verse. Some appropriate visuals include: *Pictures*: Select a picture that gives meaning to the verse. First, show the picture to the pupils as you recite the verse. Then ask them to tell what the picture shows about the verse. Explain any misconceptions your students might express. Now repeat the verse together several times. *Picture sequence*: Either the teacher or students can draw a simple series of pictures that illustrate phrases of a Bible verse. For example, for Isaiah 45:22, "Look unto me, and be ye saved, all the ends of the earth; for I am God, and there is none else," use drawings of eyes, a cross, a world globe, a number 4, the word GOD, and a circle. *Flashcards*: Make Bible verse flashcards by printing the Scripture reference on one side of the card and the words, key word, or picture on the reverse side. Rotate the flashcards as you test your pupils' knowledge of the verse or reference. *Scrambled Scripture verse race*: Select a verse that the students know from memory or one you wish to teach them. Print each word of the verse on individual strips of suede-backed paper (one inch wide and long enough for the individual word), making a double set of word strips. Before class begins, place two easels and flannelboards in front of the room with chairs underneath. (The pupils can use the chairs to hold the word strips.) Put the individual word card at one corner of the board. After the verse is taught (or reviewed), assign two pupils to unscramble the verses. These pupils should stand in the back of the room and after the signal "1-2-3-GO" walk to the easels and begin reassembling the word strips so that the verse is arranged in the correct manner. The first pupil to arrange the verse correctly wins. Repeat this procedure as long as interest and order are maintained.

Use visual aids? Teacher, catch the vision of multisensory education and use visual aids prayerfully and carefully as you lead precious souls to Jesus Christ, helping them to grow in His likeness.

Audio and Visual Resources

Books

Doan, Eleanor L. *Visual Aid Encyclopedia.* Glendale, Calif.: Gospel Light Pub., 1967.
Getz, Gene A. *Audio-Visuals in the Church.* Chicago: Moody Press, 1959.
Manson, Alice H. *Visualize to Vitalize Christian Teaching.* Los Angeles: Cowman Pub., 1959.

Bulletin Boards

Junior Bulletin Boards. Scripture Press Pub., Inc.
Le Bar, Mary. *Pre-School Bulletin Boards.* Scripture Press Pub., 1969.
Paper Arts and Crafts. Framingham, Mass.: Dennison Manufacturing Co., 1963.
Weseloh, Anne Douglas. *E-Z Bulletin Boards.* Palo Alto, Calif.: Fearon Pub. Inc., 1959.

Equipment

Full-Color Picture-Sound Programs by Canon for use with the Phono-Viewer Show 'N Tell.
Phono-Viewer Show 'N Tell, by General Electric.

Flannelgraph

Rogers, Fay. *How to Use Flannelgraph.* Cincinnati: The Standard Publishing Co., 1950.

Plastic Flip Charts

The Key. Grand Rapids: Christian Reformed Pub. House, Oct. 1968 (pp. 71-73). Nov. 1969 (pp. 69-70).

Puppets

More Paper Bag Puppets. Glendale, Calif.: Gospel Light Pub. House.

Paper Bag Puppets. Glendale, Calif.: Gospel Light Pub. House.

Split/35 Filmstrips and Records

Barrett, Ethel. *True-to-Life Missionary Stories* (four grade levels). Glendale, Calif.: Gospel Light Pub. House.

12 THE FAMILY'S INVOLVEMENT IN THE SUNDAY SCHOOL

Marilyn J. Schaal

Our family unit consists of father and mother in their thirties and five normal children from ages one to eleven—the first and last are boys and the three girls are in between. Dad and mother come from Christian families and both of us have had Sunday school, catechism, and Christian day school training. Our children are getting the same training. As their parents, we see Sunday school as a wonderful avenue of giving them certain values that we believe are not obtained elsewhere. As their mother, I want to write on my views and expectations of the Sunday school for my children and hope that my Sunday school measures up to those expectations. If it doesn't, I may not be too critical because I know that the Sunday school has its weaknesses; but on looking back over my own Sunday school experience, I realize that it did good things for me.

For the three- and four-year olds, Sunday school is usually the first formal learning experience related to the Christian

---

Marilyn J. Schaal, Grand Rapids, Michigan, is a former secretary and the mother of five children.

religion as a subject of organized teaching and of social contact with other children of the same age level. In this experience the children are not only the subjects of the teaching, but they also participate realistically.

At this young age, the child is most receptive to Biblical teaching, for he shows a lively interest in stories in general and in illustrated or dramatized stories in particular. These latter methods are a real asset in captivating his attention. The young child loves hearing the same story repeated word for word and is not bored by such, but rather obtains a sense of security in knowing it will be the same.

Almost every parent can tell of occasions when reading a favorite story to a very young child, having inadvertently omitted a word or phrase, he is immediately corrected. This goes back to the psychological need for security which is found in a repetitive learning process. At this age a child can be helped to prepare for Sunday school by having the mother, or one of the other members of the family, read the next story over and over. Rather than becoming bored, he will anticipate the next event or story, and obtain more enjoyment than if he didn't know what to expect.

The young child takes so naturally to rhythm and music that this is an excellent way to begin to teach the love of the Lord in songs adapted to this age group. Here, I as a mother want to assist the Sunday school in implementing the teaching of songs in Sunday school by going over them at home and emphasizing them in the home. The songs combine simple words that can have a deep meaning to our children, and the actions help emphasize the important points. This results in teaching Biblical truths by song. Sunday school is the logical place for teaching our children the ways of the Lord and of reinforcing the background and beliefs of the home. As Christian parents we vow to rear our children from the cradle on to walk through life in a godly manner. It is important, therefore, to begin as early as possible with our children and to continue especially through a child's formative years. The Sunday school as an added force fortifies the home in its teaching, and the home must support and back up the Sunday school in its program.

It is further essential that both home and Sunday school teach the same eternal truths. Therefore a visit to the Sunday school or a conference with the teacher on this point of curriculum will be mutually beneficial so that home can work in closer cooperation with the Sunday school.

A Sunday school class is usually a young child's first experience in a controlled social situation. Here he is brought together with his peers for the purpose of religious education in an enjoyable, compatible, and noncompulsory group experience. The children cooperate with one another in marching to songs, giving their offerings, and learning the lesson, as well as listening to and taking part in the stories. They often go into family experiences, and a wise teacher uses this as an opportunity to show how the love of God affects them in their daily living.

Young children are most grateful for small kindnesses. Additional interest can be kindled by the use of attractive stickers on their papers. If used as a reward, the teacher's imagination can almost surely find a reason for each child receiving one. My home needs to cooperate and openly display these awards. We use one side of our refrigerator for our display panel. We need to give our pleased commendation; and if such an award is missed by one of my children, I can work in conjunction with the teacher in assisting him in getting the lesson. This may demand attention to a particular child, but the sacrifice of my own interests and time for this child will bring a reward to the child and me of togetherness and better understanding.

When a child is absent—and I must see to it that he is not absent without good reason— he can be touched by receiving a "we missed you" card. This emphasizes the fact that he is an important member of the class. Upon his return the next week he will feel welcome rather than perhaps uneasy for having been "out of the action." We try not to force our children to attend Sunday school but rather try to make it seem so worthwhile that they will not want to miss. At this point again we have the right to expect that our Sunday school is worthwhile in every phase of its operation.

The Sunday school printed material is a valuable help for

the family as a devotional aid. Because a family has a differing age group of children, the usual solution is to aim toward the middle or lowest age bracket. This often has the effect of boring the older ones. Ideally, just one child and his parent could use the Sunday school material at least one evening during the week. Perhaps the ideal time for this is at the bedtime hour for a private devotion period, as a child is more at ease to discuss his real feelings when he knows he will not be overheard or interrupted by other members of the family. In a family with several children it is increasingly difficult to set aside a time for the much needed solitude with each one, but the need for such a period cannot be stressed too strongly. To set a value on this time so that it is reserved for their time alone with each other and the Lord is to demonstrate to the child his importance to you, your emphasis on the spiritual aspect of his life and yours, and your support of the Sunday school program. Our lives are so wound up in daily needs and this world's interest that when it comes to dealing with our children, physical strength and patience often evaporate before we get to the spiritual. It is my real concern that my children receive the individual attention so necessary for development as a confident and truly spiritual person. If a family is so blessed as to have grandparents, it should be recognized that they are a most valued asset in the family unit. Children definitely benefit from knowing another generation. They also may see their parents from another approach—that they really were someone's children also. In our family, godly grandparents have been a real aid in giving the children the individual attention they need and crave. When a grandparent spends time with a grandchild, he can often give the parents a new and fresh approach to the child's personality. It is easy to talk about our beliefs, but to be effective we must exhibit the living truths daily to be convincing to our children.

A good time for using the Sunday school lesson is at the Sunday noon dinner hour. Several good things can be accomplished there. One is that all will have a part in discussion, and even if there are several papers on different levels each child in his turn can present the message of his paper or lesson.

Children who do not attend church or Sunday school are always welcome in our Sunday school. Our children can encourage their neighborhood friends to attend with them. If the visiting children, however, are from a family not used to "dress up in Sunday clothes," a lesson in empathy might possibly be to have our children wear school clothes rather than their newest and best. In this way we can illustrate that God does look at our hearts and does not judge us primarily on our outward appearance. We show respect, however, for God and His place of worship by being neat and clean.

The family can be a real ice-breaker for the Sunday school by inviting the neighborhood children into our home and having a Bible story hour as an inducement in channeling these children into our Sunday school.

As the pupil becomes older, the emphasis shifts from the Bible stories to drawing from the Biblical lessons practical applications to the young person's life. The earnest teacher in the Sunday school and the mother in the home prepare diligently for this age group, as these children are adept at seeing through insincerity. Good opportunities must be sought on the part of the parent and teacher for openings where discussion is encouraged and the fruits of those discussions not piously commented on but related to daily living. Many times these honest, seeking young ones will open up freely in such a situation, particularly in the informal environment of the home. We may not seem shocked or censurious when at those times our children or young people are honest enough to tell us what lies on their hearts. This is the way to keep the lines of communication open between us parents and our children.

The Sunday dinner hour can also be used by the parent to inquire about the happenings in the Sunday school class; and, hopefully, the young person will open up to an expression of interest. Invited friends, especially the nonchurched, will profit by such informal family discussion. Care of course needs to be exercised in the kind of persons we invite.

One subject that bears attention on the part of Sunday school teacher and parents is the matter of prayer. The well-prepared and spiritually minded teacher will have guidelines to draw on in class, such as involving students in devotions. She will realize that some are more shy and withdrawn than others, and will use every resource to obtain the maximum benefit from the lesson, which sometimes will be carefully structured and at other times informal and guided by the discussion of the moment.

In the area of good rapport and discipline, parents can help immensely by making it clear to the child that they are firmly behind the teacher in expecting the child to respect and cooperate with the teacher, not out of a legal demand but rather out of a loving interest. Too many classes, ruled by an iron hand, have been ruined and a profitable lesson lost because of either too strict or too lax an attitude on the part of a teacher who didn't really love or work with the class. At this point the Sunday school needs the loving cooperation of the family.

Our family needs to give appreciation within its walls, and that must extend to the Sunday school teachers and staff also. All of us know the tremendous lift we get when we receive a sincere "thank you" for a job well done. Yet how often do we express appreciation to the Sunday school teachers for the many hours of preparation and frustration they encounter while contributing to the religious development of our children? Write a simple note to the teacher at the end of the Sunday school year, expressing your realization of her sincere efforts. Take time also to tell the teacher when a particular lesson has made a more meaningful impression on your child. A tangible token in the form of a book or picture will be a treasured reminder of your appreciation. Parent appreciation will be an added incentive to the teacher to stay at the task when it is difficult and may also have the effect of easing the recruitment difficulty of your superintendent. After all, teaching is a voluntary assignment and the rewards are meager, except when one considers that she is serving God in this capacity.

Family life today reflects the general laxness of morals and the busyness of each individual going his own way. The result is a lack of heart-to-heart intimacy, and any bearing and discussing of one another's problems and hopes may eventually fall by the wayside. Therefore, a contact for our children with a dedicated religious teacher is to be valued.

God created us with an innate desire to be wanted and loved. Children need attention, care, and love to give them a sense of security and well-being. When a mother is missing from the home at the time children come in from play or school, this element of security is missing. In our attempts at providing security we must not buckle under easily and automatically at the expense of not being present when we are needed because we are out of the home working. We should beware of the mistaken thought that we are giving our children a better life by providing them with luxuries that our Lord tells us are not necessary and probably even unwise at the time. Our hearts permit us to be swayed possibly because we didn't enjoy all these extras when we were children, or perhaps we are trying to compensate for the lack of desired affection in earlier years. We hear all around us via advertisements, "Let's get back to the basics." Let's start, rather, with the basics of our religious convictions when our children are very young and carry them over to the worthwhile basic of life by concentrating our time and effort at home to teach them abiding values by our own examples. This will be a basic value that will be of assistance when they are in Sunday school and throughout their lives.

Our children must be taught in the home a reasonable obedience if they are to react responsibly to the authority of the Word of God and the teacher in Sunday school. There is love in discipline and oftentimes one can get through to a child by "we can't permit you to do this because we care about you."

There are times when we can explain the reasons why we require obedience on a certain point, but there are as many or perhaps more times that it doesn't help. Then the firm, loving approach must follow.

If at all possible, however, attempt to lead the child to a right choice. There is always a difference in opinion between the generations, but try to remember your feelings some years ago. When a problem does arise, approach it with an open mind so that it can be remedied without serious consequences. Recognize that as parents we are not infallible and the fault may lie in ourselves. Parental influence in educating children is powerful. Let us make our relationships God centered so that our home is one which is happy and spiritual, and where love, peace, and intimacy are prevalent.

With a stronger, Christ-centered background, the child, having had a sound Scriptural training, will be better equipped to go into adulthood as a secure, confident Christian.

In these days, every effort for the preservation and upbuilding of our children is worthwhile. Therefore, this writer cannot emphasize strongly enough the importance of Sunday school education beginning at the three- and four-year-old level, continuing up through the grades and going on through high school into adulthood. Our children do not receive so much religious training as to reach the level of oversaturation. A well-planned and well-operated Sunday school, together with our other religious agencies, will be a strong force in building a well-rounded Christian life for the child. Our homes need to support our Sunday schools to become such an influence.

Life is not becoming easier these days, particularly for the Christian, and now is not the time to retrench or discontinue the Sunday school with the values it can teach. As we increase our mission emphasis and orientation in Sunday school, we need to realize that it must also continue to be vital to our own children. Because the home is the heart of loving education and devotion, the mother and father try to make that home more loving and secure. Paul's words in Philippians 4:8 are goals for us to keep constantly before us, endeavoring to surround them with the things and thoughts that are "loving, true, honest, just, and pure" and leading them to think on these things.

The Sunday school helps our homes by emphasizing these same values and goals to our children. For this reason, I want the Sunday school to be one of the best places for adequate training. Therefore, I pledge myself to its existence and improvement. God bless our homes and Sunday schools.

13 PRAISING THE LORD WITH MUSIC

Carole Zinger

> *Sing unto him, sing praises unto him;*
> *Talk ye of all his marvellous works.*
> *Glory ye in his holy name.*
> —Psalm 105:2, 3a

Music is an important aspect of the Sunday school program; for music, too, can communicate the Word of God and its truths to the children. The function of the Sunday school is to train the children in the ways of the Lord, in evangelism, and in Christian living. Music can be one way of accomplishing this by means of the hymns and choruses we teach.

Music has always been an important avenue of spiritual expression, as illustrated by some of the songs recorded in the Bible. Exodus 15:1-19 tells of the song Moses sang when Israel was delivered from the Egyptians, and Deuteronomy 32:1-43 tells of the song he sang when the Israelites were

---

Carole Zinger, Grand Rapids, Michigan, is an elementary music teacher for the Grand Rapids Christian School Association. She is also active in Sunday school work both as a teacher and music leader.

delivered from their wanderings in the wilderness. Of the songs recorded in the Bible, notice how the psalms played an important part in the life of David, of God's people, and in the temple worship. In the New Testament in Luke 1:46-55 one of the great songs recorded is that of Mary, in which she praises God for being chosen to be the mother of Jesus. Still another song is found in Matthew 26:26-30, which tells of Christ and His disciples singing together at the Last Supper. The redeemed in Revelation 5:9, 10 are joined in joyous, triumphant song in heaven. Music, as in the days gone by, is an important part of the Christian's life today and hereafter.

Music can be a beautiful expression of one's faith. The Sunday school pupils may be taught the historic Christian faith through songs that express our beliefs. In contrast, too many wrong and even heretical ideas seep into our thinking through songs that are not correct in their teachings of truth and life. There are various ways in which music can teach children the Word of God. This can be accomplished by combining music and a sacred text, by instrumental music that reminds the children of songs learned previously, and by using music to set the mood for worship. All these ways can be of spiritual value for both the teachers and pupils.

Martin Luther made this statement concerning the value of music: "Next to the Word of God, music deserves the highest praise. The gift of language combined with the gift of song was given to man that he should proclaim the Word of God through music."

Just as the Biblical songs enveloped the minds and lives of people of Biblical times and Luther in his day caught the importance of music in teaching truth, we too must strive to use our music in the Sunday school today for that same purpose.

Music assists children in self-expression and helps them gain knowledge and understanding of Biblical truths; and, therefore, it develops their Christian principles. Because songs can stay in the minds of pupils for their entire life we should be sure that these songs will say something meaningful and worthwhile. The younger children have limited ability to express themselves, and so the words of a song are important for their self-expression and Christian witness. Words set to music are often impressed upon the mind of the children so they gain lasting knowledge from the music learned.

The songs that the children sing can be used throughout the entire Sunday school period. Opening devotions should always include singing. Have them sing a prayer, a welcome, a birthday greeting, or whatever fits the occasion during any part of the Sunday school period. Songs should be sung as part of the lesson. The younger children especially enjoy doing this. A song with motions can tie in with the lesson, giving variety to it and helping the pupils to remember the lesson more effectively. The Sunday school period should be closed with prayer and with a song that correlates with the lesson. Then the children leave Sunday school with a tuneful message on their lips. This is a positive reinforcement of the truths that we want stored in their hearts.

There are many songs that are suitable for the various age groups. The preschool children should be taught songs that they can relate to and that have a simple melodic line. Choose songs that are not too symbolic but are simple and clear in declaring the truths of Scripture. The children in this age group do not think in abstractions or symbolism, so do not choose songs that are confusing, meaningless, or beyond their vocabulary or musical depth. Appropriate songs could include "Jesus Loves Me," "Can a Little Child Like Me?", "Jesus Bids Us Shine," "In Our Work and in Our play," "Into My Heart," "Praise Him, Praise Him, All Ye Little Children," "Away in a Manger," and so forth. Children in the preschool age group also enjoy songs with motions. Even the simple motions that you may think up add excitement to the songs for these children.

The children in the primary and intermediate departments can relate to songs dealing with prayer, Bible stories, sin, repentance, and Christian living. This age group will also enjoy some of the motion songs. Some such songs include "Holy Bible, Book Divine," "Stand Up for Jesus," "What a Friend We Have in Jesus," "Holy, Holy, Holy," "Shepherds Watch Their Flock," "Lord, Teach Us How to Pray Aright,"

"Long Ago Within the Temple," "Oh, Leave Your Sheep," and many others.

The junior high and senior high groups are inspired with songs that deal with nature, the love of God, thanksgiving, and personal experiences. A few examples of such songs are "Jesus Calls Us," "O Master, Let Me Walk with Thee," "Amazing Grace," and appropriate choruses. Today many new songs are being composed and they "turn on" this age group. If you use any of these you will need to be selective, making sure that they teach the right doctrinal and spiritual message.

The adults of the Sunday school can sing a great variety of songs. They will receive a blessing singing along with the younger pupils if the group meets together. They also will be blessed by all the hymns and choruses that may be chosen by any age group. To be identified with the new generation, they should enthusiastically participate, trying not to be negative or critical but helpful so that appropriate song books and songs are used.

Always choose songs that are reverent and respectful for the above groups. Try to foster a good attitude in your choice of songs and by the way they are sung. Do not cheapen your singing by permitting shouting, yelling, stomping, or by attempting to put your songs to popular tunes. Strive to honor and praise God by the songs and by the way you sing them.

There are a number of good books that can be used in the Sunday school. Use different song books from time to time and even sing without books occasionally. Collections such as *Hymns for Youth*, *The Children's Hymnbook* (both published by the National Union of Christian Schools and Eerdmans Publishing Company) offer many fine songs for the Sunday school. However, do not ignore the official church hymnbook. Let the children explore it and sing from it often.

The use of the metrical index in our hymnbooks is an exciting and interesting fact for the children to discover. The young children can be taught this without much difficulty. The metrical index of tunes has numbers listed such as 8787, 4848, and that indicates the number of syllables per line and that the tunes listed under each number are interchangeable. The children, for example, can then sing "Abide with Me" to the tune of "God of Our Fathers."

Music is one of the helpful aids in worship. It demands the use of our mental capacity to absorb the content of the song and our emotional response to the melody and rhythm of the song. With this learning concentration it then becomes a personal experience for all present. There are many types of songs we can use to worship God in our Sunday schools: hymns, choruses, songs with descants, rounds, canons, and gospel songs. A hymn is a song that gives expression of our praise and adoration. Hymns have been used by Christians down through the centuries since the early Christian church, and the Psalms are an integral part of these hymns. A descant is a melody that is sung with another melody but one that is usually higher in pitch. A canon is a song with two or more voices that enter the singing at regular intervals and imitate the first voice in strict rhythm. A round is a song that is sung by different groups who enter the song one after another and who may continue to sing the song over and over. A gospel song is a simple restatement of the Scriptural good news and tells what it has done for man. Gospel songs have a place in the repertoire of the Sunday school. The main function of the song service is not for musical training but for worship. Music must have something vital to say, and for some people certain kinds of music may not do this as well as others. Our endeavor is to reach everyone with songs that are musically sound and theologically correct and meaningful.

It is a God given blessing to be able to sing and to demonstrate many things through our singing. We can show His righteousness, holiness, love, mercy, and justice, and in that way praise and honor Him. There are numerous other ideas we can transmit through music: Bible stories, doctrine, theology, ethics, love, joy, peace, missions, and discipleship. It is truly a joy to be able to teach children to sing sincerely and to help them understand and mean what they are singing. We praise the Lord through these songs expressing gratitude, joy, praise, dedication, repentance, and love—all for the glory of God.

There are a number of practical methods that can be used to teach a song and also many ways to use these songs after they are learned. We should try to lead the children in singing what is musically correct while remembering that our basic goal is a spiritual one. One way to learn a new song is by following these steps: (1) have the pianist play the melody of the song, omitting the harmony; (2) have the children hum or sing the syllable "lu" as the pianist plays the song; (3) have the children speak the words of the song; (4) have them sing the words with the music. It is profitable to have pictures that will go along with the song or motions. This will assist the pupils in learning the song and build their eagerness. Use your imagination when teaching new songs as well as when you are singing the familiar ones. Work on new ways to sing the songs and have new motions for the students to try. The more enthusiasm the leader shows, the more enthusiasm the children will display in return, and the more eager they will be to sing. If the leader suggests some new ideas to accompany a song but does not show that he is excited about it, the students will sense his mood and follow his example.

Encourage the Sunday school to sing correctly and expressively while capturing the spirit and mood of a song. Have the class speak the words of the song at times to help them grasp the meaning. Then help them express with their voice inflection the words they are singing with their lips and tongues. Expression comes more easily if the songs are memorized and the pupils are not concentrating so hard on reading the words. While in the process of capturing the mood of the songs be careful not to base the songs on emotional demands for emotion is very changeable. Give the children a joy they can carry in their hearts while keeping emotion in proper balance with the content of the Sunday school material.

Help the students always to sing fervently and earnestly but not overly loud. Loud singing does not imply good singing, and it could damage some of the young children's voices. Let some of the older children and adults provide the volume for the singing.

Variety in the music and in the way the music is sung is

one of the key motivating factors in the singing of the Sunday school. At times try having two groups sing—one group on the stanza and another on the chorus or alternate phrases. Have the teachers sing a stanza of a song once in a while. For variety have the primary or preschool pupils sing for the rest of the Sunday school. Have one group be an echo, waiting in another room or in the balcony and singing its part at the proper time. Have musical signals that will tell the children what to do. The younger children enjoy this and will make a game out of it. For example, have a signal directing the class to sit or stand or come to order or to dismiss. Another idea you may try is to piece several songs together and sing them through without an interlude, like a medley of songs. Have the children sing along with records once in a while. It is better, however, if the record is recorded by children's voices. The Sunday school pupils will imitate the voices on the record, which will result in better singing. Incidentally, if it is a new song they will learn it quickly.

Keep your music peppy and moving—do not put your pupils to sleep by slow singing that drags. The children will remember the songs better if the tempo is kept lively. Have a "hymn of the month." Sing it every Sunday and have the children memorize it thoroughly. Let the classes take turns choosing it. For a change of pace tell the story of a hymn occasionally. The children will enjoy hearing about the blindness of Fanny Crosby or about the life of Frances R. Havergal. Hymn writers like Isaac Watts, Charles Wesley, and John Newton have had interesting lives; so allow the children to find other songs in their books written by these same men. Some good books from which to obtain information on hymn writers are: *The Story of the Hymns and Tunes*, by Brown and Butterworth; *Stories of Great Hymns of the Church*, by Silas H. Pain; *Stories of Hymns We Love*, by Cecilia Margaret; and *Famous Hymns with Stories and Pictures*, by E. H. Bonsall.

Have a talent week every month or two and have the classes take turns being in charge. That class or individuals from that class can then perform for the entire Sunday school. They may sing or play their instruments or be grouped into duets, trios, quartets, or sextets. Always keep the music Christian in concept, for music in the Sunday school is really Christian education; but also let the children have fun with it at the same time. In that way they will be more willing and able to accept the message in the songs. They will learn to treasure them and will keep them in their hearts.

Preludes are good at the beginning of the Sunday school hour. Play familiar songs that are suitable and stimulating. A few examples are "Onward, Christian Soldiers," "What a Friend We Have in Jesus," "Safe Am I," "Immortal, Invisible, God Only Wise," "This Is My Father's World," and so forth.

Since the Bible lesson is the main emphasis, select music that correlates with it. Just choosing hymns and other songs at random is not good. Be sure that the songs fit in with your Bible lesson. You may make a few remarks that tie in with the song and lesson, but do not preach or moralize. The song will often speak for itself and usually in a beautiful and poetic way. This selection takes time and preparation but is essential and worthwhile. It should be a "must" in the teacher's total preparation of the lesson. It is, however, a good motivating factor to let the children choose a few songs each Sunday. They all have their favorites and they enjoy choosing them for the entire Sunday school to sing. You could even ask them if anyone has a song that will help tell the story for that week. This gives them a feeling of being involved in the lesson in a tangible way.

The music leaders and accompanists also play an active and important role in the musical function of the Sunday school. It is not necessary for a music leader to be an accomplished musician. The Sunday school is interested in the spiritual growth of the children that attend, and there are many helps and aids to assist those who are serving as a music leader in the Sunday school. It is not even necessary always to have a piano or organ to accompany the singing. Much singing can be done a cappella if need be. If you have a difficult time finding a starting pitch without a piano, obtain a pitch pipe or some tuned instrument to help you.

The Sunday school pianist or organist should give leadership to the singing of the group. Give a short introduction and do not play as a follower but as a leader with zest and enthusiasm so as to urge on good singing. For a change it might be well to have some different instruments accompany the singing. Many of the children play instruments in school bands now, so let us make use of them. Show these pupils that they can serve the Lord with their talent, and encourage them to continue their study because they now have an incentive and goal which is to serve the Lord with their talent. Many people in Bible times utilized their instruments and talents for the praise and glory of God. They were used for various occasions: public ceremonies, battles, and religious festivities. These instruments are classified into three main categories: string, wind, and percussion. Some of these instruments were the harp, psaltery, sackbut, dulcimer, pipe, flute, organ, horn, trumpet, cornet, bells, cymbals, and timbrel. The European word for *guitar* has the same root as the word *harp*. The guitar has certainly become a popular instrument recently and many young people are proficient in playing it. Let some of these pupils accompany the singing from time to time. It attracts their interest as well as helps them be actively involved.

An interesting area that could be explored in the Sunday school is the use of rhythm instruments. A tambourine, hand drum, triangle, rhythm sticks, or others could be used to accompany the singing by almost anyone. Allow the children to create their own accompaniment; or have them play the steady beat, strong beat, melodic rhythm, or the introduction. The various songs we sing can readily be used with several rhythm instruments as an accompaniment.

It should be our constant prayer that the children retain as much of the material presented to them in Sunday school as possible. It has been said that people retain only ten percent of what they hear, and fifty percent of what they see. On the other hand, they retain seventy percent of what they say and ninety percent of what they do. Music has the pupils "saying" and "doing," and so through the channel of music the children can retain much of that presented to them.

Work and pray that the Lord will dwell richly in the lives and hearts of all of us as we use the gift of music to instruct and teach our children the ways of the Lord. Colossians 3:16 says, "Let the word of Christ dwell in you richly; in all wisdom, teaching and admonishing one another with psalms and hymns and spiritual songs, singing with grace in your hearts unto God." William Hendriksen in his commentary on Colossians tells us our every thought, word, and deed should be guided by Christ dwelling in us. He further states that the word *psalms* refers to the Old Testament psalter, the word *hymns* refers to songs of adoration and praise to Christ found mostly in the New Testament, and that *spiritual songs* are sacred songs of all kinds that were not in a direct manner praising Christ. They all must be sung, however, with thanksgiving in our hearts. This is our challenge—to guide and help all who are in Sunday school so they will have a song of gratitude and thanksgiving in their hearts as they journey through life, loving and serving the Lord.

14 SUNDAY SCHOOL MANAGEMENT

James P. Hoekenga

Words have a way of hitting people. The mentioning of a single word will elicit very diverse impressions in a small discussion group. When we mention the word *management*, we are sure that the members of a group of Sunday school teachers would have different reactions.

Some individuals might associate management with what is repressive, stern, and surely restrictive in nature. Others, who hold to the option "I will do my own thing," might feel that any kind of management or supervision in the Sunday school would stifle their imagination and original style. Thus they resent supervision or just ignore controls and rules and go their own way. I have known other teachers who say, "Just allow me to take care of my own class in my own way and I won't bother anyone else."

While there may be some valid reasons for individuals holding the above reactions to some degree, basically they are wrong and if carried to the ultimate will result in chaos in the school. We interpret management in the Sunday school orga-

---

James P. Hoekenga, Grand Rapids, Michigan, is the director of alumni relations and college information at Calvin College.

nization to mean a program of control, jointly agreed upon by the staff and properly applied, which will make possible effective teaching and bring honor to God. Management is not something negative, but a framework of operation that makes the positive possible and meaningful.

The management of a Sunday school is more than rules and regulations to control conduct, attendance, and other aspects of mechanical operation. Management includes the provision for and the use of proper facilities, team-planning by the staff of an interesting and challenging program of instruction, the adequate training of teachers, communication with the consistory and membership of the church about the Sunday school, and teaching students to be orderly and to handle the Word of God with reverence in discussions. In fact, proper management is exactly what the apostle Paul had in mind when he admonished the early Christians to do all things in proper order. Not to have good organization, management, and control is to do a disservice in this area of important and vital kingdom work.

After we take note of the essence of good supervision we hope to turn in greater detail to the various practical aspects of the Sunday school supervision.

The proper supervision and organization of the Sunday school is the key to the success of this institution in the church. This may seem to be a rather broad statement, but thoughtful reflection will convince one of its pointed truth. Any educational organization loses a major share of its effectiveness and in some cases much of its power because of poor organization and supervision. Effective teaching requires at least a minimum set of standards and regulations if it is to be carried on in a sustained and purposeful manner. It is indeed regrettable that in many a Sunday school not even the common decencies and rules of etiquette are demanded of the pupils. Such insubordination on the part of the pupils coupled with a general lack of respect for sacred things and the disadvantage of inadequate facilities, makes teaching almost impossible, no matter how well-meaning and consecrated a teacher may be. A first rate Sunday school, therefore, requires good organization and supervision if it is to hold a respected position within the organizational life of a church.

Supervision must always be secondary to the fundamental and primary duty of the school, which is teaching the truths of Christianity, the Christian life and practice as they are found in the Word of God. Supervision therefore must never be an end in itself but must always contribute to the higher goal. If the rules and regulations of an organization do not sustain, enlarge, and develop the more fundamental aim of real teaching, they lose their effectiveness and in most cases become a hindrance to purposeful teaching. It is safe to say, therefore, that every phase of supervision must be purposeful; and before any regulation is put into effect, it must be weighed and tested for its workability. There are far too many rules passed in the Sunday school organizations that are unworkable or are enforced only by strong pressure and guarded control.

A constant changing of rules and supervision causes the pupils to receive the impression that the Sunday school is poorly administered and that rules mean very little. In some cases, the attitude on the part of the pupils seems to be that the pupil may determine the rules and how effective they should be. The condition in one Sunday school seems to be reflected in the words of one youngster when he said, "In our church the teachers just can't control us." You say there is something basically wrong when such a spirit exists and you are absolutely right. In the first place, there is a wrong attitude toward the work and function of the Sunday school, demonstrated by a superficial and flippant attitude concerning spiritual things. In the second place, the insistence upon rule and order in the house of God is lacking. This second factor may be due to a poor enforcement of the existing regulations. It may be due to unwillingness to enforce regulations that are badly in need of revision. Some organizations are so bound to the tradition of the past that they seldom change an institutional regulation, even though they know it is impractical and unworkable. Let us not forget that we must respect tradition but not worship it.

We should be careful to note that good rules and regulations do not necessarily guarantee a strong organization.

The key to any policy is the carrying out of its demands; and in the case of the Sunday school, this means the individual teachers. Their lack of wholehearted cooperation in the enforcement of policy will cause the collapse of any program that has been mapped out, no matter how good it may be. Many a Sunday school has from all outward appearances the framework of sound control and supervision but is ineffective because the teachers relegate all the disciplinary problems and decisions to the superintendent. Some of them apparently seek to impress the pupil with the idea that all reprimands and matters of conduct are for the "chief" to care for and that it is well for the pupil to steer clear of that authority. They sometimes add the remark: "Of course, for my part, I don't care; but don't tell anyone I said so." Such encouragement of a lack of respect on the part of even a few teachers is the deathblow for sound supervision.

Having briefly discussed in a broad way the importance and purpose of supervision, let us turn to a more detailed discussion of the various phases of the problem of organization and supervision. We will aim to cover the following matters: (1) some of the particular problems that are faced by most of our Sunday schools, (2) the problem of teacher supervision, (3) the problem of pupil supervision, and (4) some concluding suggestions.

Particular problems often raised

One of the most distracting problems of supervision in almost all of our churches is that of space. Many churches just do not have enough rooms for meetings; and as a result, too many classes are scattered around the auditorium. Even adult classes would have a hard time concentrating under such conditions. Teachers either talk so softly that the students have a hard time hearing what is being said, or they are forced to talk so loudly that competition between teachers increases as the period progresses to the point where each one is trying to out-shout the other. It would appear that there are several possible alternatives. First, how about changing around the departments by placing the primary department in the auditorium and putting the older classes in the individual rooms usually occupied by the younger children? Another possibility would be the consolidation of the upper classes into a young people's group. They would have their own officers and several supervising teachers who would assist in the handling of the details of organization and week by week take turns leading the discussion. The older groups have much in common, and their consolidation into one group in a smaller room will free space for other groups or allow for more freedom of space if more than one group should have to continue to occupy an auditorium.

A second contributing factor in supervisory control is the time of meeting. Immediately after the morning service is not the best time for sustained interest and concentration. In some churches Sunday school is held before the morning worship and in other places it is held in the afternoon. If the Sunday school session continues to be held after the morning service, it would seem that the entire period, including opening and closing devotions, should not exceed forty-five minutes as a maximum. If the meetings are well organized and start promptly, it would seem that that length of time would be sufficient. Most Sunday school teachers will admit that the attention of the class is good for the first fifteen minutes and fair up to twenty minutes, but after that it is poor most of the time. Cannot we teach a lesson in fifteen or twenty minutes? Or does it take us so much longer because we are unprepared? Let us stay with the subject under discussion, not drift all over the horizon, and then drive the point home in a practical and interesting way. Remember, too long a session causes all kinds of related problems to arise.

Another problem of supervision is linked up with the support given the organization by the parents. Needless to say, many discipline cases are due to the fact that the pupil realizes that the parent is indifferent to his conduct in the Sunday school. He may have heard the Sunday school slandered or severely criticized by the father or mother. The problem therefore becomes one of arousing the proper attitude among the parents and in turn having that attitude permeate the attitude and conduct of the pupils. It will probably be impossible to sell all the parents on the Sunday school and its program. Our task, however, is not to account for adverse attitudes on the part of some parents but to suggest ways to remedy the same. From the standpoint of the Sunday school, four suggestions can be given to improve the situation: (1) Give regular publicity to the work and program of the Sunday school at frequent intervals. (2) Show the parents that the school is well organized and that supervision is thorough—never let the Sunday school become a mere time-filler for a period of time each Sunday. (3) Every Sunday school organization should have a project to work for, pray for, and claim its interest. Such a project might be the support of a missionary, a national worker, a home evangelization project, Bible distribution, or other service projects. Make your Sunday school an active and working organization. (4) Every part of the Sunday school program should be coordinated, such as class organization, the systems of promotions and awards, a record system, and the papers used. To put it simply and briefly, the Sunday school must be organized and supervised so that it is of credit to the local church. This may take years to attain, but it is well worth the effort.

Another question faced by many Sunday schools is that of trained or qualified teachers. Because good organization is dependent on capable teaching, we should not accept everyone for teaching simply because she has volunteered. Any person who really wants to teach but is not qualified should study and try to develop the ability under qualified guidance before taking over a class. Throughout the entire week the children are under trained and qualified teachers; and then if they are placed under incompetent direction on Sunday, it is no wonder that many problems arise. In all justice to the Sunday schools, the pupils, the parents, and respect for God's Word, we must insist on high standards for the teachers we use. Let it never be said, "Anyone can teach Sunday school."

Supervision of teachers

Having discussed briefly four particular problems that confront most Sunday schools, let us turn to the matter of teacher supervision. This phase of supervision is most difficult and at the same time most important for the superintendent.

It is imperative that proper teacher supervision be carried on constantly because many teachers lack adequate training and experience. Even if all the teachers were highly efficient, supervision would still be necessary. Most teachers in the Sunday school desire more training and need the aid of intelligent and sympathetic direction. Much can be accomplished by in-service training. If we have teachers who are not qualified for their work when they begin, careful supervision is the only means of maintaining anything like reputable educational standards.

Supervision is also necessary if all forces of the Sunday school are to be directed and correlated to the end for which the school has been established. A school at its best requires not only that each teacher be successful in doing her work well, but that all the teachers work together as a unit. To secure this cooperation requires a directing mind which is capable of seeing the necessity of unity of effort and also capable of securing it.

Supervision also furnishes a stimulus to regularity and uniformity of work. There must be uniformity within the differences that exist. There is room for individuality, but it must always be in the framework of policy and code of conduct and performance commonly agreed upon.

Effective supervision calls for a careful diagnosis of each teacher's strong and weak points. Some teachers will need little direct supervision and others will need a great deal. The type of supervision will vary greatly as the case demands. The problem of teacher supervision is a challenge to every superintendent.

There are several principles that should govern all supervision:

1. Help should always be given where it is most needed. We might also add that it should not be given before it is needed. There is such a thing as learning by personal experience. As long as the teaching of a beginning teacher is not definitely injurious to the welfare of the students and the

school, and which in the end will not harm the teacher, much can be learned by a teacher "seeing it through." However, we must be quick to add that even this apparent independence on the part of a beginning teacher must be carefully supervised from behind the scenes.

2. Supervision must always be purposeful and systematic. Only such control can assure an amount of uniformity and thus allow both teachers and pupils to know where they stand.

3. Commendation should be given when deserved. It is so hard for most of us to pass along a compliment. On the other hand, commendation should not be given indiscriminately. It may be misleading and detrimental to a beginning teacher. Instead of giving assurance, it may give a false feeling of confidence. For those who really know themselves ill directed, compliments tend to give the impression that the superintendent is insincere or even incompetent. Be honest and frank, yet sympathetic and human at all times.

4. Criticism should be constructive. All must learn what they should not do, but negative criticism often deteriorates and is easily misinterpreted.

5. Matters of routine should be mechanized as much as possible to allow for the fullest measure of real guidance. Supervision can quickly become nothing more than mere routine checking. Uniformity must be insisted upon as a means of acquiring a better organized group and the maintenance of rules that are fair for all. Plans of uniformity are conducive to good order, to economize time, and will result in habits of cooperation and fellowship.

6. Successful supervision should allow for initiative and originality, and allow for the fullest possible amount of freedom. This will stimulate the feeling that all are engaged in a common problem and all have a definite stake in the work at hand. Such freedom of expression and work must never be so individualized that other members of the staff are annoyed or feel the common rights and standards of all are being bypassed.

7. Finally, make as few rules as possible. The rules one has should be good and few, thus assuring less possibility of

confusion and a clearer understanding of the regulations that do exist.

A very important part of supervision is the development of proper attitudes on the part of the staff. The proper attitude assumed toward any work is considered one of the first requisites for success. Work in the kingdom is no exception and demands even more in this respect than other types of work. If teachers are engaged only because no one else can be found for the work, or if they volunteer only out of a sense of duty for the church, they will probably not succeed. There must be a full appreciation of all the phases and problems of the teaching function. It is the responsibility of the superintendent to inform all beginning teachers concerning the challenge that they face. Then from time to time, either directly or indirectly, he should call to the attention of the staff the pertinent problems. It is so easy to get into a rut and simply take the attitude, "Well, we have always had that problem in this church and no one has ever solved it; so I guess it is no use for us to go into it either."

Teachers must not only assume a religious attitude but also a professional attitude: there must be a certain pride in one's work. Too often Sunday school teachers practically apologize for the fact that they are teachers. Others seem to indicate that a mere devotion to the work is sufficient to indicate the presence of a proper attitude. The teacher should approach his task not only with consecration but also with an intelligent and scientific attitude.

Another element in teaching supervision is the development of good will among the members of the staff. Because the Sunday school meets only once a week and then for only a short period of time, a spirit of unity among the teachers is often lacking. When they are together they are busy either with the children, or—as is the case at teachers' meetings—they are engrossed in regular business or the study of the lesson. Is not a good share of social fellowship and informal contact on the part of the group desirable? To put it differently, are we so busy just doing the job that we don't take time out to enjoy each other's social and spiritual fellowship? Have your teachers had an outing or a luncheon recently? Do you have a dinner at the end of the church year or at the opening of the fall activities for all engaged in the work of the church, including the Sunday school teachers? Is there a definite attempt to spread the feeling that we are all coworkers in one large family for a phase of work in the kingdom?

Important in teacher supervision is the matter of determining which teachers fit in best on certain levels and with the various classes. Many a teacher would be far more successful if he taught on a different level and with a different type of class. Some teachers have taught for years on the same age level. Even if we grant that they are successful, for the sake of the teacher it might be well for her to change. An entirely new age level presents a new challenge and tends to keep the teacher more on her toes, makes teaching fresh, and creates new interests. Furthermore, some Sunday schools do not rotate the teachers but allow one teacher to progress with a class for a period of years. While such a practice might work successfully at times, far more evidence can be presented to show that in the end it is detrimental for both the pupil and the teacher.

Undoubtedly one of the most difficult tasks of supervision is the discipline of a teacher. The release of a teacher from her duties should be done only upon rare occasion, and then with as much tact and Christian grace as possible. There are cases where a lack of cooperation exists to such an extent that it is harmful for the spirit of the other members of the staff and gives the wrong impression to the pupils. Such a release from duties should not be effected without warning and previous consultation. A good time for processing a change is at the beginning of each Sunday school year, when other administrative changes are made. In case the problem is so serious that the superintendent does not wish to be responsible, the matter should be taken to the committee of the consistory that has jurisdiction of the matter. In any event, unbridled criticism of the policies of the Sunday school and a disregard of the rules should not be permitted to continue unchallenged. Sunday school morale will suffer where there is a disregard for authority and where a spirit of common purpose is missing.

It is well for any teacher group to arrange for joint meetings with other teacher groups in the area. An exchange of ideas and the discussion of common problems are not only enlightening, but encouraging to those engaged in kingdom work. Teachers should take time out for these extra contacts. In fact, teachers should be impressed with the fact that Sunday school teaching is more than just a Sunday task. Meetings on weekdays and extra personal preparations make it one of the most challenging and time-consuming tasks in the church. Any task in the church if properly executed calls for many more hours of work than the mere time of meeting.

The teachers' meeting is an important function in the educational program of the church. It can be inspiring, helpful, interesting, and businesslike without losing its informality and social character. Rather than discuss all the implications, here are listed a few rules and suggestions:

1. Have a set time limit for the meeting. Long, drawn-out meetings are a deathblow to successful teachers' meetings.

2. Get business under way quickly and execute it with dispatch. Teachers' meetings should not become the church gossip club or a debating society.

3. Have a definite period of time for the business part of the meeting and have much of the preliminary work, such as suggestions of proposals, worked out in advance by the officers and standing committees.

4. Insist on a high percentage of attendance. There are Sunday schools where certain teachers attend teachers' meetings so infrequently that when they attend they are of little help. Such people should quit teaching, for they are not doing a complete job as a teacher and their measure of participation is unfair to the rest.

5. The superintendent should have the business of each meeting well planned. Although there should be room for discussion and expression of opinion, no one should be permitted to monopolize the discussion.

6. Before a teacher begins active teaching in the Sunday school, she should attend several meetings to become

thoroughly familiar with the work and function of the organization.

7. It might be well to set aside a meeting in each quarter for the discussion of reports, special problems, child psychology, change in policy, or the planning of a program.

8. There should be an encouragement of teacher participation in the discussion of the lesson. Too often the blotter system is employed: all the teachers do or are allowed to do is "soak in." The instructor gives all the facts and no one dares to raise a question for fear she may be frowned upon.

9. In order to arouse the interest in the teachers' meetings many groups have resorted to the practice of having the teachers take turns in leading the discussion of the lesson. Be that as it may, whoever is in charge should spend time in telling the teachers how to teach the lesson. More time should be devoted to the practical application. So often that part of the discussion is tacked on because all the time has been spent in arguing minor points. Interesting highlights and historical background material should be brought in. The Sunday school must stress the vital truths of Christian experience and living, and that can be done only if the discussion in the teachers' meeting is so conducted. Teachers must feel that they really miss something if they are not at teachers' meetings. They must be taught such approaches, explanations, and applications that the lessons will live for them. Their teaching can rise no higher than the inspiration and spirit they possess. The problem of laxity in teacher attendance and flagging interest will disappear when a Sunday school conducts vital, interesting, practical, and helpful teachers' meetings. That means that the exposition of the lesson must not be a mere story telling. It may be well for the first part of the meeting to be carried on by departments, so that each group discusses the lesson from the standpoint of age level and interest. Then for the closing devotions and business let all the teachers meet together.

10. All teachers' meetings should be permeated with an air of true spirituality. This will tend to give a feeling of importance for the work being done and of unity of action. Then many of the petty matters that otherwise take up time and cause hard feelings will be obviated.

Supervision of pupils

Since we have stressed the supervision of the teachers and the need for a good organization of the Sunday school, it has become evident that if a measure of success can be attained in the program we have thus far outlined, most of the problems connected with pupil supervision will be cared for. In our discussion of this phase of supervision, we will attempt therefore to remain largely constructive and present some of the factors in the objective ideal of a well-controlled student body.

The present practice of segregating boys and girls into separate sections is responsible for many of the control problems we face. This whole idea is foreign to children of school age, who are accustomed to coeducation. The family unit is built on the coeducational basis, and all of society in our modern day includes the participation of both sexes in common enterprises. Such segregation, it seems to us, is unnatural. In the case of boys it leads to boisterousness, and on the part of the girls to incessant talking and visiting. We believe that the presence of both groups in the class would have a wholesome effect on each other and at the same time would cut down on the number of classes that are necessary.

If the control and supervision of pupils are to be effective, the spirit of the school must be high. If standards are set high, the individual conduct will be high. Regular attendance, a worshipful attitude, a reverence for sacred things, respect for authority, and a general interest will obtain in proportion to the level of the spirit of the organization.

It is our observation that many Sunday schools fail to start on time, with the result that everyone, including the teachers, seems to take the whole matter of getting down to business very lightly. Getting started on time can be likened to starting off in step for a parade.

It is a rule of child psychology that you can make a child do almost anything provided he is interested in the thing he is asked to do. We believe that it is well for us to take a page out of the psychology book. When the instruction given is presented uninterestingly, haltingly, and at times with an evidence of poor preparation, it is understandable that the students become listless and cause discipline trouble. Part of the matter of interest is also to be found in offering variety in the opening exercises and in the other items in the schedule of activity. "The same old thing in the same old way" cuts down on interest. The message of the Sunday school should always be the "Old, Old Story"; but its presentation and the worship conducted in connection with it should be vital, living, and varied in order to appeal to youth.

Earlier in our discussion we mentioned the fact that parental backing was very essential to the success of a Sunday school. That parental backing is not without signficance in the matter of control of pupils. Obviously most parents are totally unaware of the conduct of their children while in Sunday school. If the pupils were aware of the fact that now and then a report was given to the parents on their work and conduct, and that in the case of a serious infraction the home was to be contacted, there would be far more care on their part to stay in line. Often parents are not aware of a situation until the trouble is almost beyond repair. Keep the work and problems of the Sunday school before the parents and convince them that the work is worthwhile and necessary. In case we are dealing with unchurched pupils, this is a good "in" to the family and a way of getting them involved in Sunday school also—and the entire family should be involved in the Sunday school.

All children like to work for awards. An important element in pupil control and supervision is a good system of awards, a variety of contests, and due commendation for work accomplished. Some Sunday schools are very careless in such matters as attendance records, memorization work, and discipline merits, with the result that awards are carelessly given with little regard for accomplishment and practically everyone gets something just for being present. Since there is nothing to incite effort or competition, interest lags and an "I don't care" attitude begins to prevail. Then trouble begins.

As we have indicated directly and indirectly so far in our discussion, there are a number of reasons for discipline trouble. Crowded conditions, unskilled teachers, uninteresting and poorly adapted general exercises, an accepted fashion of disorder, a lack of understanding of the significance of good order, poor meeting time, and a host of other matters all play their part in the discipline problem. The best way to tackle the problem would be to devote a complete and separate business meeting to the entire question, analyze the local situation, set up ideals, see if the plan fits the aims, set the pattern for the attack upon the problem, and clearly define the responsibilities of all. Then pledge the group to see the matter through and plan on a period of time to make the changes necessary. No one rids the human body of disease overnight. And the cultivation of real control takes time. The control instituted must be natural, human, and tolerant to a certain point, but firm, fair, and consistent. Usually the children do not defeat the standards of discipline in the Sunday school; but the teachers do so by an ineffective administration of, or by a disinterest in, the regulations. Teachers should never seek to be popular by being easy and overly tolerant.

The matter of discipline control is not something that is automatic. It is clearly an educational problem. It cannot be solved by the use of methods inconsistent with the nature of the problem. Control cannot be automatically superimposed upon the school. Such methods will fail. Right conduct has to be learned as well as anything else. What has to be learned must be clearly presented and incentives to learn have to be provided. Self-respect, a sense of duty and obligation, respect for the rights of others, and reverence of God and His house are all involved. These constitute motives which must be acquired by the child through experience in the environment where such motives control the conduct of others. This learning takes place day by day and week by week, thus calling for a special measure of persistence and patience.

Concluding suggestions

The closing suggestions we wish to make do not fall strictly within the scope of supervision. Since supervision, however, is dependent upon so many factors, some of the following suggestions have their ultimate bearing on our subject.

1. Try to work out a series of topics for study that do not overlap the work of any other group in the church or the Christian day school in the community. Surely there is room for a repetition of material given, but the way it overlaps often leads to confusion.

2. Because the Sunday school sessions are a week apart and from the standpoint of the child have little continuity, shouldn't the lessons be arranged according to topics or truths that are complete units in themselves instead of trying to teach a continuous story of some period of Biblical history?

3. Why not include studies in your curriculum in the history of Christian missions for a season, or great heroes of faith, or the study of Christian truths as they apply to our age? Wouldn't the interest increase both on the part of the teachers and the pupils? Wouldn't the matter of supervision and discipline take on a new light?

4. Finally, it is our firm conviction that teachers must read more, study child psychology, attend clinics or joint sessions with other teacher groups, and discuss common problems. Or if you live in southwestern Michigan, we urge the teachers to take a course in the evening at an institution such as the Reformed Bible College. Not only will the teacher be improving her teaching, but will also acquire knowledge that will be of lasting benefit.

Teaching Sunday school today is a greater challenge than it has ever been before. With day school teachers using modern tools, facilities, and techniques, and with TV programs presented very professionally, and with magazines filled with color and interesting articles, the average nonprofessional teacher in the Sunday school faces overwhelming odds, humanly speaking. Yet the challenge to bring the truth of God as taught in Scripture interestingly, seriously, devotedly, and inspiringly has never been greater nor demanded more. All supportive means must be employed to undergird the teacher. Good management or supervision will go a long way in creating a climate for instruction which can be helpful and make teaching effective. Above all, remember that effective supervision calls for the exercise of every Christian grace and a constant reliance on prayer for strength from above.

15 FROM THE EDITOR'S SCRAPBOOK

The alert leader will constantly be on the lookout for materials that will be useful through the years. Each in his own way collects items, bits of poetry, seed thought gems of wisdom, and suggestions which others have found helpful and then passes them on to whoever wishes to pick them up and make them his own. Some like pithy sayings or lines of poetry to write on a chalkboard; others find pictures gathered through the years and filed until the right occasion brings them out of hiding and back into circulation, a good treasury that increases in value as the resources are built and kept.

Because through the years there have been frequent requests for helps in studying the Bible and for a constitution, these two areas of study are included. The constitution, at best, is only a sample and will need change and modification to suit the local situation and the modern complexion of the Sunday schools or church schools or education programs. But it is a basic operational document. The balance of the material is indeed a potpourri gathered through the years and included here in the hope it will serve a good purpose to each of you.

MY BIBLE

My Bible is bound with a scarlet cord
  That reaches from cover to cover;
    It tells of the blood of the cross of Christ,
      And ties it all firmly together.

In shadow and symbol and type, I find
  Jehovah, the Christ, my Savior;
    In Pentateuch, history, and poet's page,
      And prophecy, minor and major.

So bright is the red of the Gospel cord
  As it stretches from Matthew to John;
    So crimson the line that has tied my heart
      To the heart of the Father's Son!

Here, Peter takes hold of the binding strong
  And he fishes for souls of men;
    There, Paul weaves a tent of the crimson stuff
      While he tells the old story again.

But John pulls the cord to unveil the face
  Of the One whose blood was shed,
    And I fall at His feet, for now I know
      Why my Bible is bound in red.

                                  —Anonymous

The Use of the Bible in the Sunday School

Because the Bible is the core of the curriculum in the Sunday school, it needs to be studied and known by the teacher so that the lessons can be applied to life in the way Scripture wishes. We take for granted that although some teachers may lack training in methods of teaching and professional expertise in teaching, they are at least well versed in the Bible. We may even overrate our staff on this count; therefore, our knowledge of the Bible and how that knowledge should be used is the subject of this part of the chapter.

One always begins with certain assumptions. When it comes

to the Bible, we believe (1) that God has spoken definitively and lovingly in His Word, clearly revealing His will so that if we study it we will know that will and be able to teach others what it is. (2) He calls each one of us to herald and make His Word known, as both the Old Testament (Isa. 43:10) and the New Testament declare (Luke 24:48; Acts 1:8). (3) God has given us a strategic place for teaching His Word, for living and witnessing for Him in the institution of the Sunday school. Have you ever thought of how many nonprofessional people are gathered around His Word on Sunday morning, teaching it to literally thousands of people from smallest children to aged adults?

To be effective in the use of the Bible in Sunday school, we need to know at least three things: (1) how to read our Bibles effectively, for as teachers of it we need to be somewhat expert in its contents; (2) how to read our Bibles from the slant of being able to witness effectively—in other words, our method is basically found in God's message; (3) how to apply its message to ourselves first of all and then to the others to whom God leads us.

In reading the Bible, there are certain rule-of-thumb observations that we will have to remember.

1. The Bible is God's Book, that is, it is His revelation, His message of love to us. As such, it gives accurate, inerrant knowledge about Him and His world, our purpose and destination, and the way to live according to His will.
2. The Bible is the church's Book, used by the church for worship and instruction, for guidance and inspiration, for living according to His will, and for witnessing.
3. The Bible is a readable book—read it aloud as coming from a living person.
4. The Bible is a spiritual book—with a worldwide, spiritual message.
5. When you are reading a Bible:
    a. *Mark it.* Obtain a copy of the Bible that you wish to use for reference. Use different colored pencils or ball-point pens to mark specific passages that trace through ideas; for example, salvation texts in red, promise texts in purple, and mission texts in green.
    b. *Memorize it.* Develop the habit of learning key pas-

sages and verses that will be of help in working with people and for your own enjoyment and spiritual upbuilding.
  c. *Meditate on it.* Spend time faithfully concentrating on the chapters and verses you are reading. Let the Holy Spirit speak to you through the Word as you are contemplating its message for you that day and for the days and work ahead.
  d. *Mention it.* The message of the Bible must not only enter your soul, but it must be channeled through your soul to others.

When dealing with the Bible, there are certain principles that you need to follow. Read it prayerfully with the bent of mind or commitment to find God's directions for your life as you witness for Him, and God through His Holy Spirit will guide you. Read the Bible with this purpose in mind: "Lord, show me from the Word how you wish me to witness."

Read the Bible and use it each step of the way, truly believing that God means what He says when He makes promises about the power of His Word.

Read the Bible for methods. As you go along, ask the question as to how God would have you go about witnessing or teaching, with the slant that you are searching for methods as to how God wishes you to carry out His program.

In studying Scripture, keep certain passages or texts in mind that deal with the nature of the Word and the use you are to make of it. Some of these passages are: II Timothy 3:16, 17; Psalm 119:105; I Peter 2:2; Ephesians 6:17; and Acts 28:23.

Anyone that takes Bible study seriously will find that Satan will try to hinder at every turn of the way. To read and use the Bible effectively, there will have to be a mental attitude toward it that makes one desirous of spending time with it. Our time is so often taken up with the things of earth—not wrong in themselves, but not conducive to spiritual thinking and living. Because the Word does not clamor for attention, we are in danger of neglecting it. We should set time aside and develop patterns of habit for reading and praying and looking for doors to utilize the fruits of our reading and prayer.

Try to bear in mind that Christ came into the world to do the will of the heavenly Father (John 5:30). In doing that will He was revealing to us that He came to seek and to save the lost so that they could again be brought into living fellowship with God through the Holy Spirit and into communion with one another in the church. Since Christ has commissioned us (John 20:19-23; Acts 1:8) to be His representatives, we will have to study the Word to know His will, and in knowing it show our deep love for our loving God by serving our fellowman in love. Will you accept that challenge?

NOT I, BUT CHRIST

"Not I, but Christ," be honored, loved, exalted;
"Not I, but Christ," be seen, be known, be heard;
"Not I, but Christ," in every look and action,
"Not I, but Christ," in every thought and word.

"Not I, but Christ," in lowly, silent labor;
"Not I, but Christ," in humble, earnest toil;
Christ, only Christ! no show, no ostentation;
Christ, none but Christ, the gatherer of the spoil.

—A. A. F.

I remember running over the hills just at dawn
one summer morning and, pausing to rest in
the silent woods, saw, through an arch of trees,
the sun rise over river, hill, and wide green
meadows as I never saw it before.

Something born of the lovely hour, a happy mood,
and the unfolding aspirations of a child's soul
seemed to bring me very near to God. . . .

—Louisa May Alcott

CONSTITUTION OF THE SUNDAY SCHOOL

Article 1. Organization

The Sunday school is an important auxiliary of the church and is therefore organized under the jurisdiction of its consistory and controlling board.

Article 2. Purpose

The purpose of the Sunday school is to increase the pupils' knowledge of the Word of God; to instruct them in the application of the Bible for everyday Christian living; and, where the pupil is not a Christian, to secure, through the Holy Spirit, and faith in Christ, a living commitment to Jesus Christ.

To develop in the children of the Sunday school a love for missions and a desire for personal witnessing for the Lord Jesus Christ.

To make the Sunday school an effective, evangelistic arm of the church, thus making it a witnessing agent in the community of which the church is a part.

Article 3. Executive committee and officers

The Sunday school shall be governed by an executive committee consisting of the officers of the Sunday school, which are the superintendent, assistant superintendent, secretary, and treasurer. Nominees for the position of superintendent and assistant superintendent are to be presented by the consistory and elected by the teachers, the superintendent to serve a three-year period. Other officers are to be nominated and elected by the teachers at the first business meeting of the Sunday school year, with these officers serving from the time they are elected until the subsequent election the next year; and the fiscal year shall run for the same period.

Article 4. Teachers' appointments

Teacher nominees selected by the teachers and superintendent or by the superintendent and presented by the superintendent shall be approved by the consistory. Final placement is to be made by the superintendent. Appointments shall be for one year, and reappointments shall be made at the discretion of the executive committee and/or the consistory. Teachers shall be required to attend all teachers' meetings, except with due notice of absence to the secretary or superintendent.

Article 5. Teachers' meetings

The teachers shall meet weekly or biweekly on a stated evening to discuss and receive instruction in the lesson for the following Sunday(s). The instructor shall be selected by the teachers and presented to the consistory for approval. A business meeting shall be held on the last meeting night of each month. The executive committee shall meet during the week prior to the business meeting on a date set by the superintendent.

Article 6. Collection

At each session of the Sunday school, a collection shall be taken for the general expenses of the Sunday school and for support of special causes. Collections from the special sessions of the Sunday school shall be appropriated as deemed necessary by the executive committee.

Article 7. Amendments

The constitution, excepting Articles 1, 2, and 7, may be changed by a two-thirds vote of the teachers, subject to the approval of the consistory.

BYLAWS

Article 1. Duties of officers

Sec. 1. **Superintendent**—The superintendent shall have charge of the Sunday school and arrangement of classes and whatever other tasks fall within his administrative domain. He shall preside at all public meetings, take charge at teachers' meetings, exercise authority in matters of the executive committee, function as the liaison officer between the Sunday school and the organization committee of the consistory, and submit an annual report to the consistory on the work of the Sunday school.

Sec. 2. **Assistant superintendent**—The assistant superintendent shall assist the superintendent in all his activities and, in the case of the superintendent's absence or incapacity, shall fill his office.

Sec. 3. **Secretary**—The secretary shall record minutes of the business meetings, keep teachers' attendance records of weekly meetings, and carry on all necessary correspondence.

Sec. 4. **Treasurer-librarian**—The treasurer-librarian shall have custody of all funds of the Sunday school, make all necessary disbursements as approved by the superintendent, and distribute teaching materials each Sunday. The books shall be audited by the consistory auditing committee at the end of each fiscal year.

Article 2. Duties of the executive committee

Sec. 1. The executive committee shall have final authority in the case of discipline of pupils. Regarding discipline of a teacher, the executive committee through its superintendent shall only recommend to the consistory. Final exercise of such discipline shall rest with the consistory.

Sec. 2. The executive committee shall appoint all committees necessary to promote the work of and interest in the Sunday school.

Sec. 3. The executive committee shall insert news items

concerning the Sunday school in the church bulletin at least once a month, hoping thereby to stimulate congregational interest in the Sunday school.

Article 3. Qualifications and duties of teachers

Sec. 1. **Qualifications:** The teacher

- A. Must be a member in full communion of the church.
- B. Must have a true knowledge of the Bible and doctrine.
- C. Must have ability to teach, be able to communicate that teaching, and maintain order.
- D. Must have love for the cause of instructing children through the medium of the Sunday school.

Sec. 2. **Duties:** The teacher is

- A. To prepare each lesson faithfully.
- B. To give due notice to the superintendent in case of expected absence.
- C. To give the superintendent three weeks' notice in case of resignation.
- D. To attend teachers' meetings regularly. Two consecutive absences from teachers' meetings for reasons not acceptable to the executive committee make a teacher subject to dismissal two weeks after official notification.

Article 4. Duties of appointed committees

Sec. 1. **Mission committee:** at least two people shall compose this committee. The Committee shall

- A. Obtain speakers and make all necessary arrangements to have speakers every three to six weeks.
- B. Notify superintendent and treasurer of Mission Sunday date.
- C. Periodically place in the bulletin information regarding the programs of the Sunday school.

Sec. 2. **Special promotions:**

The executive committee or the superintendent shall appoint special committees as needed.

THE CHILDREN

Bring them into the sunshine,
Out of the gloomy night;
Out of perilous places,
Bring them into the light.
Bring for the love of the Master,
He, Who Himself did give.
Teach them how His compassion
Encompasseth all that live.
Show them the pathway of duty
That upward their feet may tread,
That "Of such is the kingdom of Heaven"
May still, as of old, be said.

—Carmen Vander Veen Liddick
Houghton, New York

—It is related of Alexander the Great that being asked how it was that he had conquered the world, he replied, "By not wavering."

—After praying to God, there must be action by man to find God's answer.

THE SOUL OF A CHILD

The soul of a child is the loveliest flower
   That grows in the Garden of God;
Its climb is from weakness to knowledge and power,
   To the sky from the clay and the clod.

To beauty and sweetness it grows under care,
   Neglected, 'tis ragged and wild.

'Tis a plant that is tender but wondrously rare,
  The sweet, wistful soul of a child.

Be tender, O gardener, and give it its share
  Of moisture, of warmth, and of light,
And let it not lack for thy painstaking care
  To protect it from frost and from blight.

A glad day will come when its bloom shall unfold,
  It will seem that an angel has smiled.
Reflecting its beauty and sweetness untold,
  In the sensitive heart of a child.

—Author Unknown

From *A Source Book of Poetry* by Al Bryant. Grand Rapids: Zondervan Publishing Co., 1968

THE HEART OF A CHILD

The heart of a child is a scroll,
  A page that is lovely and white;
And to it as fleeting years roll,
  Come hands with a story to write.
Be ever so careful, O hand;
  Write thou with a sanctified pen;
Thy story shall live in the land
  For years in the doings of men.
It shall echo in circles of light,
  Or lead to the death of a soul.
Give here but a message of right,
  For the heart of a child is a scroll.

—Author Unknown

From *A Source Book of Poetry* by Al Bryant. Grand Rapids: Zondervan Publishing Co., 1968

THE SOLITARY LAMB

"For Israel slideth back as a backsliding heifer: now the Lord will feed them as a lamb in a large place." Hosea 4:16

It is what is peculiar to sheep, we know, that they continue under the shepherd's care: and a sheep, when driven into solitude, shows itself by its bleating to be timid, and to be as it were seeking its shepherd and its flock. In short, a sheep is not a solitary animal; and it is to sheep and lambs almost a part of their food to feed together, and also under the eye of him whose care they are.

—John Calvin

BECAUSE I HAVE BEEN GIVEN MUCH

Because I have been given much, I too must give;
Because of thy great bounty, Lord,
Each day I live, I shall divide my gifts from thee
With every brother that I see
Who has the need of help from me.

Because love has been lavished so upon me, Lord,
A wealth I know that was not meant for me to hoard,
I shall give love to those in need,
Shall show that love in word and deed;
Thus shall my thanks be thanks indeed.

—Grace Noel Crowell

THE BOY AT THE CROSSROADS

He stood at the crossroads all alone
   The sunrise in his face;
He had no thought for the world unknown,
   He was set for a manly race.
But the road stretched east and the road stretched west,

And the boy did not know which road was the best;
So he took the wrong road and went down.
　He lost the race and the victor's crown;
He was caught at last in the devil's snare,
　Because no one stood at the crossroads there,
To show him the better road.

Another day at the selfsame place,
　A boy with high hopes stood;
He, too was set for a manly race,
　He was seeking the things that were good.
But a Sunday school teacher, who the road did know,
　Stood there and showed him which way to go;
So he turned away from the road that went down,
　And he won the race and the victor's crown.
He walks today the highway fair,
　Because one stood at the crossroads there,
To show him the better road.

DO WE HAVE TIME FOR VACATION?

There is no need for Sunday school
I've heard it said so much
I learned the stories as a child
In Christian school...and such.

We really need to get some rest
It's good to get away
At least for August let's close it down
That's just a small delay.

Next year more time seemed needed
Dinner early seemed so good
Some protested but were defeated
Few wondered if they really should.

God has told us in His Book
To work—to watch—to wait—

To bring the lost ones in
Before it is too late.

How can we tell the new one who
Just came from a Christless home
That we're closing our doors for the summer?
In Satan's path he'll roam.

And while we're rushing here and there
Viewing the wonders of our nation
Let's remember our Heavenly Father
Who never takes a vacation.

—Ruth Wells

Increasing Your Sunday School Attendance

Dr. Clarence Benson in his book *The Sunday School in Action* states that the average Sunday school has only about one-half of its land under cultivation and the other two-thirds is producing weeds and tares. There are many reasons for this situation, but there are also ways for overcoming it.

The best advertisement for your Sunday school is a satisfied group of teachers and scholars who are enthusiastic and talking about the work being done.

When the Sunday school is regulated well with properly graded classes and good management as well as devoted and talented teachers, there is a mighty incentive for pupils to take visitors with them to school. To make the visitors feel welcome and give them an incentive to come back, give them a good reception the first time they come. Make them feel welcome by introducing them by name to your class.

A competitive spirit within the Sunday school classroom through the use of contests is another method of getting your pupils to return with friends. Children enjoy contests, especially if they win. A simple badge or pin purchased from a Sunday school supply house for each memory verse learned or each time a Bible is brought along or even for the number of times Sunday school was attended can be of great help in getting children excited about returning the following week. Keep in mind, however, that you do not make this the focal point of the Sunday school or a bribe to get the children to return.

Have you thought in terms of a car race? Obtain a wall map of Palestine or North America, using your own ingenuity as to what you wish to prove. Have two students with paper cars or airplanes go from one city to another and tell one fact that happened in each city. The one who gets there first with the most correct information is declared the winner. For example, one could start at Gaza, move on to Bethlehem, Jerusalem, Sychar, Jericho (if you use a car remember there is a river to cross if you go up north by way of Perea and for that reason you may want to avoid Sychar), Gerasa, Gadara, Capernaum, and Nazareth.

There are so many other ideas you can follow in the line of creating interest: (1) house-to-house visitation (Luke 10:1); (2) stickers and attendance cards; (3) social activities and functions; (4) having your students handle and use the Bible for interesting searches.

There is also the need of enlisting the pastor for promotional work. When there are seeking souls in the community who have become interested in the Sunday school and need to learn most intently about God, Christ, sin, and salvation, enlist the pastor's help. At the same time establish a visitation and revisitation program of names of students you have obtained through canvasses, through your visitor's register, and from your students who are on the lookout for new friends as they move into the neighborhood.

—He loves each one of us, as if there were only one of us.

—Augustine

—Live to seek God, and life will not be without God.

—Leo Tolstoy

CONCLUSION

Sunday school—what an institution for teaching and spreading the good tidings of the gospel! Are you really sold on its challenge? As these pages conclude their offering of help and inspiration to you, you should pause, having absorbed their contents and learned the lessons they wish to teach, with a personal prayer of commitment to the Lord Jesus Christ that you will give yourself more wholeheartedly and lovingly to the challenging tasks here presented. Your task may be to function as a superintendent, or teacher, or simply to be constantly in prayer that God will use your work in the Sunday school to harvest and instruct precious souls who come within your range of contact. What a wonderful task He places on all of us: Some are called to greater responsibilities; others to lesser tasks, but all to faithful endeavor. Thanks be to God for giving us this work in the Sunday school and the promise of victory through Him in that work!